34   uic   £3

SHROPSHIRE HILL COUNTRY

Shropshire Hill Country

by

Vincent Waite

PHILLIMORE

First published by
J. M. DENT & SON LTD.
1970

This edition published by
PHILLIMORE & CO. LTD.
London and Chichester

Head Office: Shopwyke Hall,
Chichester, Sussex, England

ISBN 0 85033 365 2

Printed in Great Britain by
Graphic Colour Print, Emsworth 6141

To All Friends Round the Wrekin and Elsewhere

The area dealt with in *Shropshire Hill Country* is covered by Ordnance Survey one-inch maps 118, 128 and 129 or Ordnance Survey 1:50 000 maps 126, 136 and 137

Contents

List of illustrations ix
A select bibliography xi
Preface xv
Acknowledgments xvii

1 The background of history and legend   1
2 Ludlow and the Clee Hills   17
3 Much Wenlock and Wenlock Edge   43
4 Church Stretton and its hills   62
5 The Long Mynd   85
6 The Stiperstones   101
7 The district of Clun Forest   109
8 The Shropshire lass and lad   127
  Appendix *A short sketch of the geology of Shropshire hill
  country by A. W. Coysh*   150
  Index   154

List of illustrations

Between pages 38 and 39
 1 The Wrekin from Wenlock Edge *R. N. Cove*
 2 Well at Hope Bagot *M. L. Waite*
 3 Caynham: fourteenth-century churchyard cross *M. L. Waite*
 4 Ludlow Castle *M. L. Waite*
 5 Much Wenlock: the cruck house beside Saint Owen's Well
   M. L. Waite
 6 The Church Stretton Sheila-na-gig *H. Griffiths*
 7 Church Stretton from Cardingmill Valley *M. L. Waite*
 8 Acton Burnell Castle *R. N. Cove*
 9 Pontesford Hill *M. L. Waite*
10 The Devil's Chair *A. P. Wallace*
11 Old lead mine workings on the Stiperstones *A. P. Wallace*
12 Wenlock Priory: Norman arcading of the Chapter House
   M. L. Waite
13 Wenlock Priory: panel of the cloister lavatorium *M. L. Waite*
14 Rushbury: typical Shropshire domestic architecture
   M. L. Waite
15 The village green at Woolstaston *M. L. Waite*
16 A. E. Housman's 'Hughley Steeple' *M. L. Waite*
17 Jacobean craftsmanship in Wentnor church *M. L. Waite*
18 The River Onny near Plowden *M. L. Waite*
19 Gliding near the Long Mynd *J. Minshall*

20 Titterstone Clee Hill *M. L. Waite*
21 Offa's Dyke near Llanfair Waterdine *M. L. Waite*
22 'The House on Crutches' at Bishop's Castle *M. L. Waite*
23 Samuel Lee
24 Mary Webb
25 A. E. Housman
26 Clun Castle *M. L. Waite*

Maps

Shropshire Hill Country   xx–xxi
Diagrammatic geological map of the district   148–149

A select bibliography

Hilda Addison *Mary Webb*
T. C. Anderson *History of Shropshire*
J. E. Auden *Shropshire*
T. Auden *Memorials of Old Shropshire*
J. Austerberry *A Glimpse of Old Shropshire*
S. Bagshawe *History of Shropshire*
O. Baker *Ludlow Town and its Neighbourhood*
E. Boore *Wrekin Sketches*
E. W. Bowcock *Shropshire Place Names*
A. G. Bradley *The Book of the Severn*
Charlotte S. Burne *Shropshire Folklore*
W. Byford-Jones *The Shropshire Haunts of Mary Webb*
E. Donald Carr *A Night in the Snow*
W. Reid Chappell *The Shropshire of Mary Webb*
F. C. B. Childe *Cleobury Mortimer*
D. H. S. Cranage *An Architectural Account of the Churches of Shropshire*
S. Evans *History of Ludlow* and *Shropshire Days and Shropshire Ways*
R. W. Eyton *Antiquities of Shropshire*
W. J. Farrow *The Great Civil War in Shropshire*

H. E. Forrest *The Old Houses of Wenlock* and *The Fauna of Shropshire*

Lady C. Milnes Gaskell *Spring in a Shropshire Abbey*

Geology of Church Stretton, Craven Arms, Wenlock Edge and Brown Clee (Geological Survey of Great Britain)

A. S. F. Gow *A. E. Housman, a Sketch*

R. Graham *The History of the Alien Priory of Wenlock*

A. J. C. Hare *Shropshire*

C. H. Hartshorne *Salopia Antiqua*

M. Herring *Shropshire*

G. S. Hewins *Villages of the Clee Hills*

Laurence Housman *A Personal Memoir of A. E. Housman*

G. F. Jackson *Shropshire Word Book*

Henry James *Portraits of Places*

P. T. Jones *Welsh Border Country*

C. Lapworth and W. W. Watts *The Geology of South Shropshire*

J. D. La Touche *A Handbook of the Geology of Shropshire*

A Memoir of Professor Lee by His Daughter

W. A. Leighton *The Flora of Shropshire*

L. C. Lloyd *The Borough of Wenlock*

Arthur Mee *Shropshire*

L. P. Moore *A Synoptic History of the Midland Gliding Club*

Thomas Moult *Mary Webb, Her Life and Work*

R. I. Murchison *The Silurian System*

'Nimrod' *Memoirs of the Life of John Mytton*

M. Peele *Shropshire in Poem and Legend*

Nikolaus Pevsner *Shropshire*

R. W. Pocock and T. H. Whitehead *The Welsh Borderland*

Grant Richards *A. E. Housman*

F. T. Snell *The Celtic Borderland*

H. T. Timmins *Nooks and Corners of Shropshire*

H. W. Timperley *Shropshire Hills*

Transactions of the Shropshire Archaeological Society

Edmund Vale *Shropshire*

The Victoria County History of Shropshire
George L. Watson *A. E. Housman, A Divided Life*
W. W. Watts *Shropshire, the Geography of the County*
M. W. Weale *Through the Highlands of Shropshire on Horseback*
Mary Webb *Collected Works* (Jonathan Cape)
Graham Webster *Wroxeter Roman City*
Walter White *All Round the Wrekin*
George R. Windsor *A Handbook to the Capabilities, Attractions, Beauties and Scenery of Church Stretton*
John Wood *Quietest Under the Sun*
Dorothy P. H. Wrenn *Goodbye to Morning*
T. Wright *History of Ludlow and the Welsh Border* and *Ludlow Sketches*

Preface

This book is intended to serve as an introduction to a beautiful and historic countryside which has kept its unsophisticated individuality together with many of the outward and visible signs of an ancient past. Shropshire, the largest of English inland counties, is bounded by no less than eight other counties, four of them Welsh. This in some way explains its topographical characteristics and the wealth of its historical associations. *Shropshire Hill Country* deals with that part of the county lying south of the River Severn which virtually divides Shropshire into two halves. It is addressed to those readers who, even if only in recollection, are walkers or cyclists as well as drivers of cars and who have what G. M. Trevelyan called 'the longing, too often a thwarted longing, for natural beauty and the great unspoilt areas'. As in my former books describing other districts of the English countryside I have tried here to tell something of the story which lies behind what can be seen – the rich diversity of Shropshire hill country's superb scenery, its hills and woodlands, churches and castles, houses and villages – and to link the story of the past with the present so that landscape and places acquire a new meaning.

The march of what in our more optimistic moods we term 'progress' makes increasingly relentless inroads on the dignity and beauty of some of the loveliest countryside in the world, the countryside of England. Often proliferating undistinguished ugliness on its way it is destroying or irredeemably changing unique traditional features of this countryside in the interests of speed and building development. It has therefore been all the more satisfying for me to write about a part of England still preserving some of those unviolated characteristics which inspired its own novelist in Mary Webb and its own 'sweet sad singer' in *A Shropshire Lad*.

V. W.

Acknowledgments

I owe a special debt of gratitude to A. W. Coysh, Esq. who wrote the Appendix describing the complicated geology of the Shropshire hill country for this book with characteristic clarity and concision; and to my wife and R. N. Cove, Esq. who provided many of the photographs of the district.

Among the many others who have given me generous and ready help in obtaining information and material I have to thank the Society of Authors as literary representative of the Estate of A. E. Housman; the City Librarian, Birmingham Public Libraries; Jonathan Cape Ltd; the Church Missionary Society; the Rev. R. B. Davies; J. M. Dent & Sons Ltd; E. P. Dutton & Co. Inc; Canon D. F. C. Hawkins; J. R. Hayes, Esq., of the Midland Gliding Club; the Ministry of Public Buildings and Works; John Minshall, Esq.; Air Commodore L. P. Moore; J. B. Priestley, Esq.; A. L. Thomas Esq. and the staff of Shrewsbury Reference Library; C. R. Talbot, Esq.; J. C. Voysey, Esq., and the Forestry Commission; and the Executors of Mary Webb's estate. Acknowledgment is also due to Holt, Rinehart and Winston Inc. (with Barclay's Bank Ltd and Robert E. Symons) for permission to quote the lines from A. E. Housman's poems in the U.S.A. Plate 6 is by H. Griffiths; 19 by J. Minshall; 24 by courtesy of Jonathan Cape Ltd; and 25 from the Mansell Collection.

Lastly, I owe grateful thanks to many whose names I do not know but who have talked to me in their friendly fashion on the hills, along country lanes, over farmyard gates, in cottage gardens and in village inns, and from whom I have gained a deeper appreciation of this countryside of which they are so justifiably proud.

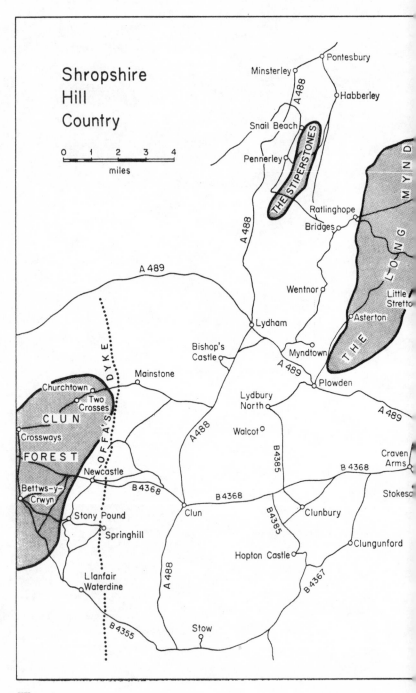

Shropshire Hill Country

To
Shrewsbury

Leighton

To The
Wrekin

Acton Burnell

Longnor

Langley

ol-
aston

Leebot-
wood

Ruckley

Much
Wenlock

THE
LAWLEY

A49

Hughley

E·D·G·E

on

CAER
CARADOC

Plaish

nurch

HELMETH
HILL

Willstone

Cardington

tretton

Easthope

HAZLER
HILL

B4371

Wallbank

ETH

Rushbury

B4378

Ticklerton

Eaton

To
Bridgnorth

cton Scott

Munslow

Beambridge

W·E·N·L·O·C·K

Cleobury
North

Westhope

Aston Munslow

Abdon

BROWN

Diddlebury

Heath

CLEE

Burwarton

Clee
St Margaret

HILL

4368

Siefton Batch

Stoke
St Milborough

B4364

Cleestanton

Callowgate

TITTERSTONE
CLEE HILL

Bitterley

Angel Bank

CLEE
HILL

Hopton Wafers

A49

A4117

A4117

Brook Row

Cleobury
Mortimer

Ludlow

Hope Bagot

Coreley

B4214

Caynham

Whitton

xxi

Chapter 1

The background of history and legend

The River Severn curving through Shropshire divides the county into two parts which are approximately equal in area but have widely different characteristics. The area north-east is for the most part an uneven plain with wide tracts of fertile agricultural land; south-west of the river is the hill country which is the subject of this book and which comprises a series of ranges – the Clee Hills forming the most easterly heights, followed in order westwards by Wenlock Edge, the Stretton or Caradoc hills, the Long Mynd and the Stiperstones. In the extreme south-west merging indeterminately into the mountains of Wales is the hilly moorland district of Clun Forest. One other height which must be included in any account of Shropshire's hills lies north of the Severn. Although it is only 1,335 feet high, the distinctive bold outline of the Wrekin rises so sharply out of the surrounding plain that it is the undisputed focal landmark of the county, the nostalgic symbol of their home country for exiled Shropshire folk and the rallying toast for 'All Friends Round the Wrekin'.

The wide difference in the characteristics of these ranges of hills is all the more remarkable because they are contained within a comparatively small area. The bare outlines of the Clee Hills are in striking contrast to the softer green wooded ridge of Wenlock Edge; and different again is the broad heather-covered moorland summit of the Long Mynd, and the harsh jagged outline of the neighbouring Stiperstones. This variety of scenery can be explained by the rich diversity of the rock formations in this part of the country, but the geological structure of the Shropshire hill country is so complicated that it needs someone trained in the subject to explain it to the layman. My friend A. W. Coysh makes it as simple as possible in the appendix at the end of the book, illustrating it with a geological map of the district.

The structure of Shropshire hill country would also greatly influence the distribution of prehistoric human settlements in the area. There are no signs of any here before the Early Iron Age; doubtless the lower slopes and valleys were so densely covered by thick forest and so treacherous with swamps that settlements below the hill crests were impossible until the arrival of those stubborn Iron Age pioneers who vigorously set about clearing and cultivating the lower and ultimately more fertile sites. On the hill tops they constructed a number of formidable forts, impressive features of Shropshire hill country which can still be traced in many areas.

The date 55 B.C. is so commonly associated with the Roman invasion that we are inclined to forget that Julius Caesar's landings in that year and the following year were only minor punitive expeditions, and that a real invasion was not attempted until nearly a century later. It was then that Aulus Plautius landed with the avowed object of subjugating the country and bringing it within the Roman empire. One spearhead of legionaries pushed northwards into Shropshire and established a centre at Viroconium near the site of the modern Wroxeter. A few years later Ostorius Scapula consolidated the conquest, but met with dogged resistance from the British fighting under the resolute leadership of Caradoc (or Caractacus as the Romans named him) who according to tradition made his final stand in or near Shropshire. Tacitus vividly describes the site of this last bitter struggle as 'on steep hills, on the more accessible parts of which Caractacus had thrown up ramparts of loose stones, while in front and down below was a river dangerous to ford'. The Caer Caradoc near Church Stretton, the other hill of the same name south of Clun and Coxall Knoll south-east of Bucknell have all been claimed as possible sites. Another suggestion is that the Breidden Hills just over the Welsh borderland more nearly fit Tacitus's description. After his defeat Caractacus fled north and took refuge with the Brigantes whose Queen Cartimandua treacherously handed him over to the Romans; but it is pleasant to recall that the Emperor Claudius was so impressed by the British chieftain's dignity and courage when he appeared in chains before him that he gave him his freedom and restored him to his family.

Britain was occupied by the Romans for something like three and a half centuries, a period as long as the span of years between the death of the first queen Elizabeth and the accession of the present queen. This is a long time and it is surprising that so little is known about the activities of the Romans in Shropshire. We know they worked lead mines in the Stiperstones district because pigs of lead imprinted with the name of the Emperor Hadrian have been found there. Roman coins have also been discovered in various parts of the county, and it seems generally agreed that some of the many fortified hill camps date from Roman times; it is even possible that a number of the earlier prehistoric camps were also modified and used by the Romans. Most important of all, of course, are the impressive remains of Viroconium, the fourth largest Roman city in Britain with an area of about 170 acres. The size of its baths and forum, and the sophisticated craftsmanship of the pottery and glass found there give some indication of its former wealth and splendour.

The Britons' long dependence on Roman arms may well have sapped some of their own former warlike spirit, and the final withdrawal of the legions in the fifth century was little short of calamitous for them. It ushered in a kind of historical twilight regarded as the 'Dark Age of Britain' because the following two

3

centuries when the Saxon hordes swooped down on the shores of England are so mysterious and ill-documented. Thus it is not known who bore responsibility for the destruction of Viroconium. One theory suggests that it was the Saxon invaders when they pushed northwards and swept to victory towards the end of the sixth century, but it is equally possible that the destruction was the work of Welsh tribesmen wreaking jealous vengeance upon the Romanized Britons whom they despised. At all events, this once thriving, bustling city became a deserted ruin and a convenient quarry for builders who must have carted away tons of invaluable remains from the site. Those inhabitants who survived the destruction of the city seem to have built up a new settlement at Pengwern where modern Shrewsbury now stands and where the loop of the river afforded them natural protection from attack.

Shropshire is border country; for many generations it was disputed land and the scene of fierce raids and counter raids. At the end of the eighth century King Offa of Mercia had pushed his territory to the western limits of the county, and the British sullenly withdrew to the unassailable strongholds of the Welsh mountains, but remained always on the watch for any opportunity to swoop down in swift marauding attacks on the Saxons' land. In order to protect the boundary of this western limit of his un-wieldy kingdom Offa constructed the remarkable Dyke which bears his name and stretches from the estuary of the River Dee to the mouth of the Wye. Parts of the earthwork may have been in existence already, needing only strengthening and repairs. Today the 168 miles of Offa's Dyke Path is a scheduled Long Distance Footpath, and although twelve centuries have naturally eroded and modified much of the earthwork, enough remains to show that the Dyke must originally have been a forbidding obstacle constructed with great engineering skill which cunningly used every natural feature of the terrain.

With the Norman Conquest came the parcelling out of great tracts of England to those who had shared with William the dangers of the invasion. Most of Shropshire was handed over to his kinsman and friend Roger de Montgomery who chose the town of Shrewsbury as his chief centre, built a castle there and was granted the Earldom of his adopted place of residence. A 'just man but severe', the earl appears to have mellowed considerably in later life; and influenced by his gentle, pious second wife he founded the Benedictine Abbey of Shrewsbury where he was buried, and restored the religious house at Much Wenlock as a Cluniac priory.

The conquest of the Shropshire hill country had been no walk-over for the Normans who met with stiff resistance led by Edric Sylvaticus, or Wild Edric. His bold strategy enabled him to besiege the Normans at Shrewsbury and to burn down part of Roger de Montgomery's unfinished fortifications there. But this success was not followed up; Edric was finally forced back, and later made peace with William, much to the resentment of some of the more stubborn Saxon patriots. A number of legends have grown up around this period of Shropshire's history. One tells how Edric was hunting over the Stiperstones and lost his way.

Wandering with a single page through the night he suddenly found himself before a lighted house filled with lovely maidens dancing to sweet music. With one of these he fell in love and he carried her off, the other dancers assailing him tooth and nail in vain. The maiden told him that if he ever mentioned her sisters he would lose her, and then would pine away himself; but he was certain that this would never be the case. They were married before all the world, and after he was reconciled to the Norman William she displayed her beauty at his court. Then after many years came a day when she angered him by coming in very late. 'I suppose it is your sisters who have kept you,' he exclaimed, upon which she instantly vanished for ever, and he died of grief.[1]

Another tradition says that Wild Edric and his lovely golden-haired wife Lady Godda were imprisoned below the Stiperstones as a punishment for his submission to the Conqueror. The lead

1 Augustus J. C. Hare: *Shropshire*.

miners of former days used to assert that at times they could hear the prisoners knocking underground and that wherever they knocked a rich vein of ore could always be found. Only when war is imminent can the couple be seen, for then they are allowed to gallop over the hills until the coming of the dawn when they must return once more to their imprisonment.

The turbulent borderland of the Shropshire hill country continued to be a threat to the Norman newcomers, and William hit upon what seemed a simple way of dealing with the situation. He settled some of his most lawless and warlike followers in the district as 'Marcher Lords', granting them privileges and any land they could conquer from the Welsh. Soon a series of castles sprang up along the border, and from these strongholds Norman lords like Roger de Montgomery of Shrewsbury, Roger de Lacy of Ludlow and Robert de Say of Clun forced the Welsh back still farther into their mountain fastnesses, and wrested more and more land from them. These Marcher Lords held sway over their particular territory like petty princes; they granted charters to towns within their domains and even appointed judicial officers. It is hardly surprising in the circumstances that such rapacious warriors were often at loggerheads with one another. The king's writ did not run in the Marchland and this convenient legal immunity led to many abuses, especially by criminal ruffians fleeing justice who could find reasonably safe refuge here by playing off one jealous Marcher Lord against another.

Trouble of another kind flared up in the area after the death of William Rufus when Robert de Belême, the eldest son of Roger de Montgomery, rebelled against Henry I. The king proved more than a match for him, and seeing his cause to be hopeless Robert fled for safety to his castle at Shrewsbury. Henry continued his relentless pursuit; avoiding the old route along the Severn valley he cut a new road over the crest of Wenlock Edge in place of the 'hollow way full of greate sharpe stones, and so narrow as scarce to admit of two horsemen abreast' which was already in existence.

As a result he arrived with his troops at Shrewsbury so swiftly that he caught the luckless Robert unprepared. More from motives of policy than of magnanimity Henry forbore to put his rebellious subject to death for treason, but contented himself with confiscating his English possessions and banishing him from the kingdom. Robert de Belême showed little gratitude for this clemency and for some years was a continual nuisance, to say nothing of danger, to the king, plotting and scheming against him until at last Henry's patience was exhausted. Robert was captured, brought back to England and imprisoned in the castle at Wareham in Dorset for the rest of his life.

The peace which Shropshire enjoyed during the last thirty years of Henry I's reign was rudely shattered at his death when civil war broke out between the rival factions supporting Matilda and Stephen in their struggle for the crown. Many of its castles like Ludlow and Shrewsbury were fortified for Matilda against Stephen. In 1138 Stephen himself led an army into the district and laid siege to Ludlow, but the castle's defender, Gervase Paganel, successfully beat off every attempt to breach its defences. Baulked in their efforts here the besieging army moved on to the castle at Shrewsbury which was also held on behalf of Matilda's cause. Both attack and defence were bitter and obstinate, but after holding out for nearly a month the castle fell. Vengeance was swift and merciless: the greater part of the garrison, about a hundred men in all, were executed on the spot. This pitiless slaughter was just one prelude to the rapine, violence and treachery which were to face the stricken populace for the remainder of Stephen's reign when men said that 'Christ and his saints slept'.

During all this time the Shropshire borderland continued to be troubled by the feuds with the Welsh who were not always content to skulk in their rugged mountain hiding places. From time to time they sallied forth to attack, often with devastating effect. One of their most threatening forays took place in Henry III's reign when they advanced over the territories of the Marcher

Lords and captured some of their fortresses. The situation became sufficiently ominous for the king himself to intervene and the invaders were driven back. In the following year Welsh resistance crumbled with the death of the only two leaders capable of welding the separate factions into a united front. Llewellyn was killed in a skirmish at Orewyn Bridge near Builth, and then in the following year his brother David was captured and brought to Shrewsbury. Here Edward I called a parliament which is something of a landmark in English constitutional history as one of the first assemblies in which representatives of the commons took part in the deliberations by legal authority.[1] David was sentenced to death and to the usual accompaniments of a traitor's death – drawing, quartering and the despatch of his grisly remains for exhibition at various strategic places as a gruesome warning to other restive subjects. The Shrewsbury parliament then moved for another session to Acton Burnell where the king was staying at the Shropshire home of his chancellor and friend, the wealthy, worldly bishop of Bath and Wells.

The century following Edward I's death was one of comparative peace for Shropshire, but there was trouble again shortly after the accession of Henry IV when he had to meet a challenge from the rebellious Percys. The king's army met the rebel forces near Shrewsbury on a site now occupied by the church and village of Battlefield; there was a fierce struggle which ended in a victory for the king. Harry Hotspur himself and a grievous number of men on both sides were killed; as one old chronicler records, it was 'one of the wyrst bataylys that ever came to Inglonde, and the unkyndyst'. The fight is well known to readers of Shakespeare who has immortalized it in the play *King Henry the Fourth*; indeed, 'by his creation of the character of Falstaff he has given us a fictitious hero who is better known than the real heroes of the fight. Those who remember little about the king or Hotspur are well acquainted with the deeds and sayings of that fat knight.'

1 *See* page 77.

With the removal of Llewellyn and David from the Welsh scene and the assumption of more direct control over the principality by the English king, the original role of the Marcher Lords was no longer needed. Despite this, some of them like the Mortimers of Ludlow became more powerful than ever and later played a decisive part in the Wars of the Roses by supporting the Yorkist cause, and thus helping Edward IV to victory at the battle of Mortimer's Cross near Ludlow. But not even the new king's debt to the Marcher Lords for this assistance deflected him from his determination to control their powers. The office of Warden of the Marches was abolished and in its place the king set up a Lord President and a Council of the Marches with headquarters at Ludlow.

To mark this new royal connection with the town the king chose Ludlow castle as a residence for his two young sons Edward and Richard, better known to history as 'the two princes in the tower'. Here the thirteen-year-old elder prince was proclaimed king on the death of his father, but the two brothers were soon moved to the Tower of London to fall victims to their uncle Richard Crookback's ambition. Ludlow later had other royal residents. Henry VII's eldest son Arthur brought his bride Katherine of Aragon to the castle for their honeymoon. Arthur died within a year of their marriage, and the Spanish widow was immediately betrothed to the king's second son, later to be Henry VIII. He in turn sent his daughter Mary to live here for a time, and probably this was one of the few happy episodes in the sad life of the wretched woman who was to go down in history as 'Bloody Mary'.

The isolated height of the Wrekin rising from the level Shropshire plain is such a commanding landmark that it was necessarily a vital link in the great chain of beacon fires which flared all over England as a warning that the long-expected Spanish Armada had at last been sighted on the first stage of its ill-fated attempt to invade this country in 1588. In Macaulay's words,

All night from tower to tower they sprang, they
    sprang from hill to hill;
Till the proud peak unfurled the flag o'er
    Darwin's rocky dales,
Till like volcanoes flared to heaven the stormy
    hills of Wales,
Till twelve fair counties saw the blaze on
    Malvern's lonely height,
Till streamed in crimson on the wind the Wrekin's
    crest of light. . . .

Although Shropshire is an inland county and so was not so
immediately involved with the threat of the Spanish landing on a
coastline, its defensive role was not limited merely to firing a
warning beacon on the Wrekin. As early as twenty years before the
sailing of the Armada the queen had ordered 'our Trusty and Well
Beloved the Sheriff and Justices of the Peace of our county of
Salop' to have five hundred able-bodied men in a state of readiness;
and among them were to be included 'halberdiers, billmen and
pikemen, together with archers and arquebusiers furnished with
their artillery'. In particular they were enjoined to take steps immediately to encourage 'the art and practice of the bow, a both
pleasant and profitable exercise which hath been too long dis-
continued, especially in our villages'. The cheapness of the bow
and its ammunition would undoubtedly have appealed to a
parsimonious sovereign who had pared the navy's strength so
drastically that a fleet of only eighty vessels was ultimately ready to
confront the Armada's 150.

In typically English fashion Shropshire's reaction to these
instructions seems at first to have been dilatory and half-hearted,
and at various musters there was often a number of defaulters,
many of them local tradesmen without the requisite weapons and
equipment. Stern measures were ultimately taken; fines were
imposed, and for more recalcitrant offenders a short period of
imprisonment was found to be a most effective stimulus to
efficiency. The situation gradually improved for other reasons,

too; a fervent spirit of loyalty and patriotism was aroused as the threatened danger grew so obviously near. The issue in 1587 of a printed *Heads of Instructions for the Muster-Master* showed that Shropshire was indeed taking matters seriously, and the county did provide a generous share of the thirty thousand men of the Midland counties who were to form a special army to protect the queen's person in the event of invasion, and who had been ordered to march to London at the first signal of alarm.

At last the long-awaited invading Armada left the River Tagus, and the news that the mighty fleet was on its way spread rapidly to England.

> Night sank upon the dusky beach and on the
> purple sea,
> Such night in England ne'er had been, nor
> e'er again shall be . . .

and in the gathering darkness beacon after beacon throughout the country, including that on the Wrekin, roared into flames and signalled its warning to the countryside all around. The Shropshire forces mustered at their various meeting points; those detailed to march to London set off for the capital, but by the time they arrived the Spanish fleet had lumbered cautiously up the Channel, and then fled northwards to be cruelly shattered and ravaged by tempest.

'God blew with His wind and they were scattered' was the bland official explanation of this astonishing deliverance, and certainly it was the weather which played the decisive part in the defeat of the 'invincible' Armada. No county in England could have heaved a greater sigh of relief than Shropshire at the end of the danger; like those of the country as a whole, their preparations were far from adequate to confront the great force the Spanish fleet might have landed and the disaster which might have ensued. This relief was well expressed in the quaint words of a contemporary Salopian chronicler when the news of the Armada's destruction reached Shropshire:

This yeare, and the 19th daye of September, being Tuesdaye,

and two dayes after the festivall daye of the coronac'n of the Queenes maiestie, and the sayde daye fallinge uppon S. Elizabethes daye, was a solempn daye in the countie, and all the people that daye keapt it holly unto the Lorde, that had Gyve' hir mtie sutch victorie, and blessid ov'throwe of the Spanishe power and hudge navy of hir enimies to the greate reioisinge of all England. God be praysid, Ame'.

The Wrekin was indeed the obvious choice for Shropshire's beacon; from its summit there is a view of practically the whole of the county. This strangely-shaped elliptical height seems loftier than it really is, rising so suddenly as it does from the plain. It is in fact not one single hill but a small range of three, beginning on the north-east with its foothills, the Ercall and Lawrence Hill, which lead over a small valley to the main height of the Wrekin. This hill more than any other is the hub of the county for Shropshire people; as H. W. Timperley expresses it, the Wrekin is as much a spirit as a hill and 'when you go to it the underlying mood or feeling is that of a pilgrimage'. A number of legends explain its origin and history; one story tells of two giants who made it as a fortress for themselves by piling up the earth they dug out of the bed of the Severn. After a time the two quarrelled and one of them hurled his spade at the other, missed him, but split the rock on the summit thus making the narrow cleft now called the Needle's Eye. Then they fought, and at first the giant who had thrown the spade had the better of the struggle until a raven swooped down and pecked at his eyes so that he shed great tears which hollowed out the Raven's Bowl on the top of the rocky outcrop called the Bladder Stone. Finally the other giant was the victor and heaped up the Ercall over his adversary's prostrate body, and there he still lies and can often be heard at night groaning and bewailing his fate.

Another legend shows the Wrekin as the work of a malevolent giant who bore a grudge against the people of Shrewsbury and set off from his Welsh home carrying a great load of earth to block up the River Severn and flood the town. After a while he lost his way, and meeting a cobbler carrying a bag of boots and shoes he asked him how far it was to Shrewsbury.

The cobbler, before answering the question, cautiously asked what he wanted there. On hearing his errand the cobbler, who thought it would never do to lose all his customers by drowning replied, 'Shrewsbury! You'll never get to Shrewsbury, neither to-day nor to-morrow. Why, look at me! I've just come from Shrewsbury and I've worn out all these boots and shoes on the road.' The weary giant in despair threw down his load, scraped his boots on his spade and returned home, leaving the two heaps – the Wrekin and the Ercall beside it – as memorials of his baffled plan.[1]

It will now be realized that even if you climb no other hill in Shropshire you must go up the Wrekin. It is an easy walk from the north-east by way of a footpath off the road running through the valley between the Ercall and the foot of the main summit. This track leads over the shoulder of the hill, through a pre-historic earthwork by way of a gap called Hell Gate, and then through the narrower opening of Heaven's Gate. Down below on the southern flank of the hill is the narrow cleft of the Needle's Eye; and the Bladder Stone with its Raven's Bowl is rather nearer on the eastern side. It is not often that such a gentle climb is so richly rewarded with such magnificent views; 'all round the Wrekin' lies that beautiful and historic landscape which witnessed the Armada beacon flaring skywards on that fateful summer night nearly four centuries ago.

After the threat of the Spanish invasion had passed by there was a century and a half of peace for Shropshire which was then tragically broken by the Civil War. Although no key battle was fought within its territory a number of skirmishes and sieges took place here which had some influence on the course of the war. Shropshire folk were predominantly Royalist, and a number of

1 Charlotte Burne *Shropshire Folklore*. A similar story is told about the formation of Cam Long Down in Gloucestershire.

castles, including Shrewsbury and Ludlow, were garrisoned for the king. Before the end of the war, however, the discipline and fervour of Cromwell's soldiers had triumphed, and every Royalist fortress in the county had been captured. Ludlow Castle was the last to submit and it fell only because members of its garrison had been bribed to induce the rest of their companions to surrender.

The consequences of the war were particularly harsh for Salopians. A large number of local men caught up in the events must have died in the fighting. From one small Shropshire village alone it is recorded that 'there went no less than twenty men to the king's army of whom thirteen were killed', and this figure might well have been comparable with casualties in other places. In addition to these tragic losses many castles, manor houses and churches had been partly or totally destroyed, and several Royalist landowners were forced to sell their estates in order to pay the exorbitant fines inflicted on them by a vindictive Commonwealth government. It is hardly surprising that the Restoration of Charles II was received with such glad thanksgiving in the county, and that one Shropshire rector wrote enthusiastically in his parish register, 'never was more cordial love and honour shown to any king than was to this exiled prince at his reception into the kingdom in all places'.[1]

The Council of the Marches had been exercising judicial and administrative functions for rather more than two centuries with varying degrees of vigour and efficiency. During this period there had often been complaints about its 'corruption, partiality, greed, delay and extravagance'. It had certainly outlived its usefulness by the seventeenth century and did not merit the expensive establishment it still maintained as a legacy from the time when royalty had kept court at Ludlow. In 1689 it was finally abolished and one of Shropshire's most distinctive links with the past was destroyed.

For the three centuries leading up to the present day the story of Shropshire has been mostly uneventful and its former distinctive

1 *See also* Chapter 7.

historical associations have given way to the all-embracing pattern of national history. Yet it is still true, as Thomas Auden remarked some eighty years ago, that the area

has maintained a character of its own all through, as is easily recognized by any who have lived both in Shropshire and in other parts of the Midlands or the north. Local life and local feeling have been, and still are, strong in Shropshire. This has arisen partly from its distance from the metropolis and it showed itself especially in the eighteenth century. Then the towns, and particularly Shrewsbury and Ludlow, had each its own season for which the county families went into residence as they now go to London. Since that period Shropshire has been brought into closer contact with the outer world, first by the rise of coaches and then by that of the railway, but it has maintained its individuality more than most counties.

No one, not even the most casual visitor to Shropshire hill country, can fail to be conscious of the diversity of this individuality enriched by links with the past, stretching down the years back to prehistoric times. The district is still relatively unspoilt, although it is certainly not isolated, lying as it does on routes to and from the industrial north and the busy holiday resorts of North Wales. Its beauty is unobtrusive and unsophisticated, and mercifully much of it is still inviolate. Yet in one unexpected way the name of the county has travelled proudly around the world. The famous Shropshire Light Infantry, raised as long ago as 1755, made the shire well known in many wars and in many distant lands, including the West Indies, Spain, India, Egypt, South Africa, France and Italy. But the real heart of Shropshire is still its hills and rivers; its castles, timbered houses and cottages; its villages and hamlets among which are some of

> The quietest places
> Under the sun.

It is a countryside which, as the historian Mandell Creighton puts it,

shows the growth of agricultural prosperity in a fertile district which became prosperous as soon as it was freed from disorder. It shows how the baronial civilization of early times gave way before the changed conditions of the country which began in the reigns of the Tudor kings. It still bears on its surface the traces of the gradual progress of English society in a region where local life was strong, and where its course had been but slightly affected by the development of modern industry, which in other counties has nearly obliterated the records of the past.

(In *The Age of Arthur* John Morris points out that "Dinlle Wrecon, the Wrekin, the pre-Roman fort .. preserves the old name of Wroxeter, Uriconium.")

Chapter 2

Ludlow and the Clee Hills

That indefatigable topographer John Leland described sixteenth-century Ludlow as 'very propre, welle walled and gated, and standeth every way eminent from a Botom'. The town's walls have long since disappeared and of its original seven gates only one remains, but its eminence still makes the place an impressive sight as you approach it from either the north or the south. An adequate description of Ludlow would need a small book to itself and the reader would be well advised to obtain a copy of the town guide which is one of the best examples of this kind of publication that I have ever come across. Here I shall merely make a personal choice of a few focal points of interest which are special favourites of mine.

If you approach the town from the south you will come to the ancient Ludford Bridge, a splendid sturdy structure which for nearly seven centuries has borne a ceaseless flow of traffic from the time of packhorse and saddlehorse, broad-wheeled wagon, stage and mail coaches right up to the present day's continuous stream of motor vehicles. Perhaps its most difficult task in recent years was during the last war when it had to support the great weight of a hitherto unknown monster, the army tank, but even that it accepted without demur. Before crossing this bridge you must turn to the left and make for Whitcliffe where Ludlow and its setting are spread out before you. In the centre of the picture is the great tower of the parish church rising to a height of 135 feet. To the left are the craggy ruins of the castle standing on its mound like the set piece of a medieval pageant. As a colourful background there is the Shropshire hill country: crumpled mountain shapes to the west; the long wooded crest of Wenlock Edge in the middle; and to the right the strange bold outline of the Clee Hills shows up against the sky. Below in the immediate foreground is the River Teme, a symbol of the many centuries which have passed by as it has flowed beneath Ludlow's two bridges.

However familiar it may be to any visitor, the approach to the town over Ludford Bridge and the vista from Lower Broad Street to Broad Gate, and then up Broad Street itself to the Butter Cross, never fails to delight the eye. The remarkable number of Ludlow's old houses can be appreciated only by a leisurely exploration on foot. Some of the more famous ones like the Feathers Hotel ('that prodigy of timber-framed houses', as Nikolaus Pevsner calls it), the Angel in Broad Street and the Reader's House near the church are obvious enough, but there are many half-hidden lanes and corners like Fish Lane, Harp Lane, Pepper Lane and Quality Square which reveal treasures just as fascinating although they are not so well known.

During the worst period of the troubled times which vexed the Marchland between Wales and Shropshire there were some thirty-two border castles in the county to maintain some semblance of precarious peace and order, and among them Ludlow's fortress on its lofty promontory beside the confluence of the rivers Teme and Corve was of outstanding importance. The castle is in fact the heart of Ludlow and was originally the reason for its existence, for the town is in every sense the capital of Shropshire Marchland. Even in its ruinous state this border stronghold is a building to fire the imagination. Climb to the top of its great Norman keep and you realize at once how magnificently the castle commands the surrounding countryside and how easily its sentinels would have been able to detect the movement of any hostile forces.

Its history is a story of bloodshed and violence; and during Stephen's reign there was a bitter feud between Joce de Dinan and Hugh de Mortimer over its ownership, a feud still further complicated by the claims of a member of the Lacy family which had originally built the fortress. One dramatic episode in the castle's history at this period deserves to be told at length. It occurred when two young knights, Walter de Lacy and Arnold de Lisle, were imprisoned here by Joce de Dinan. The prisoners were chivalrously treated with what afterwards proved to be unwise leniency; they were even allowed to enjoy visits from the ladies of the garrison, and a certain Marion de la Bruere fell hopelessly in love with the handsome Arnold de Lisle. She responded to his blandishments by contriving the escape of the two prisoners from their tower by means of a makeshift rope formed with the sheets and towels she had smuggled in.

Marion's infatuation led to further treachery. When for some unexplained reason the castle's garrison was reduced to a mere handful of knights and soldiers she sent a message to her *amoroso* inviting him to pay her a visit at night. De Lisle came, but not alone. A party of his soldiers accompanied him and while he approached the castle in the darkness they hid on Whitcliffe. Meanwhile he himself climbed into the castle by means of a rope ladder which Marion had fixed to a window. It was left hanging there and while she was engaged in amorous dalliance with her lover a small force of de Lisle's men swarmed up it, took the unsuspecting sentinels by surprise and put the whole of the sleeping garrison to the sword so swiftly that the castle was captured without the loss of a single besieging soldier. Too late Marion realized the perfidy of her lover and the enormity of her own foolish treachery, but she was determined that he at least should not profit by his double-dealing. Seizing his sword she stabbed him to death, and then as a melodramatic fall-of-the-curtain for this medieval tragedy she leapt to her own destruction from her window in the Pendower Tower.

19

On many later occasions the story of Ludlow touches national history more closely. When Edward IV was proclaimed king in 1461 he succeeded to all his father's possessions, including Ludlow Castle, and immediately set about refurbishing it and making it fit to be a royal residence. Here his two sons, later to be the tragically ill-fated 'princes in the Tower', were brought up in considerable state. The king drew up a set of strict rules for his sons' daily life in the castle with detailed instructions regarding their regular attendance at mass, their food, their education and their pastimes.

No man was to sit at table with them except such as Lord Rivers should permit, and during their meals it was ordered that there should be read before them noble stories as behoveth a prince to understand; and that the comunication at all times in their presence be of virtue, honour, wisdom and deeds of worship, and of nothing that should move them to vice.

It was in this castle that the elder brother was proclaimed King Edward V on his father's death, and it was from here that a fortnight later the two princes set out on their forlorn journey to London where they were to come to a violent end like their half-brother, three of their uncles, their grandfather and their great-grandfather – a gloomy sidelight on the transience of even royal life in those ferocious times.

The castle continued to be a kind of royal Windsor of the Midlands for the sovereign and his family. Henry VII sent his eldest son Arthur to live here, and when at the age of fifteen the prince married Katherine of Aragon they kept their court at Ludlow. Five months later he died and the unfortunate young widow was forthwith married to the exuberant Henry, then a handsome debonair young prince but already sowing his wild oats in a manner worthy of his later personality when he had become the 'big, burly, noisy, small-eyed, large-faced, swinish-looking' King Henry VIII. He in due course sent his own small daughter Mary to Ludlow and perhaps it was one of the happiest periods in the bleak life of that lonely embittered queen who was destined to die riddled with disease, scorned by her royal Spanish husband and unlamented by her people. As you stand looking down from the keep over the castle buildings you can see the beautiful Norman Round Chapel where all these tragic figures of the past must have worshipped – Marion de la Bruere whispering a secret prayer that she should see her beloved Arnold de Lisle once again; the two pathetic young princes hearing their daily mass; the dying teenage Prince Arthur kneeling beside his young Spanish bride; and the tearful nine-year-old Princess Mary, already a disconsolate figure as she implored God to restore her once again to the beloved mother from whom she had been so cruelly separated.

Turning to happier memories we can look towards the now roofless Council Hall where Milton's *Comus* was first performed in 1634 in honour of the new Lord President of the Council of Wales, the Earl of Bridgewater. Some time previously the earl's little daughter and her two young brothers had caused something of a panic in the household when they lost their way in Hayward Forest during the twilight hours of early evening, and this incident provided the slender theme for the masque in which the three children played the parts they had enacted in real life. It was perhaps fortunate that *Comus* was enlivened by some charming music by Henry Lawes which may have done something to mitigate its *longueurs*; for in spite of the beauty of its admirable songs the masque shows that Milton was devoid of any sense of stagecraft or dramatic movement. We may accept some of the tirades and monologues when we read them, but it must try the patience of the most dedicated audience to listen to the brothers calmly discussing in 160 lines whether their lost sister's virtue is threatened and whether she would be capable of resisting ravishment; and then continuing the debate for another 170 lines with the Attendant Spirit. The distinguished gathering at that memorable first performance in the castle must surely have felt that the loquacious trio might have employed their time more profitably by taking prompt and active steps to save the threatened maiden.

The castle's rival in interest, and its superior in beauty, is the great parish church of Saint Laurence. It is a building of cathedral-like proportions with a length of over 200 feet; and any detailed examination of its special features would be impossible here. Once again I prefer to make a personal choice of what I can look at again and again, always finding some new unsuspected beauty to admire. First, there are the richly carved screens, one spanning the chancel arch, another at the entry to the Lady Chapel and the third, perhaps the finest of them all, between the north aisle and Saint John's Chapel. Then there is the stained glass of Ludlow church which is justly famous. The beauty of the great east window is best appreciated with the aid of a pair of binoculars which reveals the delicacy and variety of the colours. Church windows were intended in medieval times to serve as a kind of 'poor man's Bible' for those who could not read, and they were the great majority of the populace. How often the simple townsfolk here must have looked at the east window of Saint John's Chapel which relates (with a wealth of rich Ludlow blue) the story of the 'Men of Ludlow'. This old legend is also shown in sculpture on the screen of Edward the Confessor's Chapel in Westminster Abbey and is related in Dean Stanley's *Memorials of Westminster*:

One day King Edward the Confessor was waylaid by a beggar who implored him for alms for the love of Saint John. Now, Saint John the Evangelist was the Saint whom the king venerated with special tenderness, and he drew off from his hand a ring, large, royal and beautiful, which he gave to the beggar who immediately vanished. Not long afterwards two English pilgrims from the town of Ludlow, journeying to the Holy Land, found themselves benighted in Syria. Suddenly their path was lighted up and an old man accosted them. They told him of their country and their saintly king whereupon the old man, joyously like to a clerk, guided them to a hostelry and announced that he was John the Evangelist, the special friend of King Edward, and he gave them the king's ring to carry back with the warning that in six months the king would be with him in Paradise. The pilgrims returned and found the king at this palace in Essex at a place called from this incident Havering-atte-Bower to this very day. The king received the men of Ludlow graciously, acknowledged the ring to be his, and prepared for his end accordingly.

My third choice is the robust craftsmanship of the carved misericords in the chancel. During the many long religious services of the Middle Ages the clergy were allowed one small gesture to the frailties of the flesh – the 'misericord', a device which permitted the seat of a stall to be turned up, revealing a small ledge on which a priest could lean without actually sitting down; but if he were negligent enough to fall asleep the seat would thrust him forward and thus expose his culpable inattention. The medieval carver took a special delight in exercising his craft on the underflap of these misericords, and he would produce a remarkable variety of subjects ranging from the humorous and grotesque to the satirical and ribald. Ludlow has thirty-two of these ancient stalls, and the following is a full list of the subjects carved, starting in each case from the west moving towards the altar.

North side *left facing altar*
1 Missing.
2 Heraldic Tudor roses representing the royal association with Ludlow.
3 Missing.
4 A falcon and two fetterlocks, the heraldic device of one of the Lords of Ludlow.
5 An angel sounding a trumpet.
6 A royal personage wearing a crown.
7 A deer couchant.
8 A sly satire showing a fox dressed in bishop's robes preaching to a congregation of geese. This was a favourite subject with medieval carvers.
9 The Prince of Wales's feathers. This may represent the town's association with Henry VII's eldest son, Prince Arthur, whose

heart is traditionally said to have been buried here when his body was interred in Worcester Cathedral.

10 A bishop.

11 A chained antelope, the heraldic device of King Henry VI.

12 Although this one is damaged you can still see a lively scene of a quarrel in a kitchen.

13 A mermaid with a mirror, another favourite subject for a misericord.

14 A realistic representation of a common contemporary dishonesty – short measure in an ale-house. The guilty ale-wife with her typically gay head-dress and her false measure is being carried off by a devil. As she is thrust into the mouth of hell a second demon plays the pipes, and a third reads the list of her sins from a long scroll of parchment.

15 A bat dressed in a woman's head-dress.

16 A representation of boys teasing a woman. Her expression of tearful vexation is startlingly lifelike.

South side   *right facing altar*

1 Missing.

2 The heraldic Tudor rose.

3 Missing.

4 The figure of a scholar with a scroll.

5 A drinking party; two headless men are shown supporting – from their posture almost worshipping – a barrel of ale. The side ornaments show an ale-bench, a barrel, a jug and a drinking-cup.

6 A figure with a comically tipsy expression draws ale from a barrel.

7 A griffin; the mythical monster which was said to be the offspring of an eagle and a lion, and having the head and legs of the former and the rest of its body like a lion.

8 Defaced animals and birds.

9 The horse and the money-bag beside the struggling figures

suggests that this is the scene of a highway robbery which would be a familiar experience for many Ludlow travellers.

10 A scene in a kitchen; the goodwife is contentedly warming her hands at the fireside; there is a stockpot on the logs and two pigs are strung up ready to be prepared for cooking.

11 A swan.

12 Birds, including an owl.

13 A representation of various types of elaborate female head-dress.

14 Another familiar homely scene – a man tugging at his boots with an expression of tense effort on his face.

15 Decorative foliage.

16 Possibly the representation of a gravedigger as it shows a tomb and the various implements of his trade.

It will be noticed that some of the stalls have been mutilated, evidently intentionally as heads and arms have been cut off with some sharp instrument. Four of the misericords are plain; a close examination of them suggests that their original carvings may have been removed. Possibly they were too coarse for nineteenth-century susceptibilities and suffered the same fate as two similar examples in Bristol Cathedral which were taken away in 1895. But these with baffling inconsistency were then sent to the South Kensington museum, presumably for public display.

In his poem 'Hughley Steeple' A. E. Housman wrote,

> North, for a soon-told number,
> Chill graves the sexton delves . . .

and perhaps it is fitting that it is on the outer north wall of Ludlow church that his own ashes rest behind a simple tablet inscribed with the words,

IN MEMORY OF
ALFRED EDWARD HOUSMAN
M.A. OXON.

Looking at the Clee Hills from the west it is difficult to realize that the prominent tilted cone of Titterstone Clee is not higher than the neighbouring broad-shouldered Brown Clee; but the latter is officially the loftiest point in Shropshire with a height of nearly 1,800 feet[1] and Titterstone Clee is just under 1,750 feet. The two Clees are in fact part of a short range of highlands crossed by the Ludlow to Bridgnorth road which winds over the rising upland between these two summits described by the sixteenth-century topographical poet Michael Drayton as

> These mountains of commande,
> The Clees, like loving sisters, and Titterstone, that stand
> Trans-severed, behold faire England towards the rise,
> And on the setting side how ancient Cambria lies.

On Brown Clee there are the remains of the sites of three pre-historic forts, Abdon Burf, Clee Burf, and Nordy Bank, a smaller camp on the west flank of the hill. The strange name 'Burf' is supposedly derived from a Celtic word 'bruarth', an enclosure, which is obviously connected with these earthworks. The hill can be climbed from Burwarton, or more steeply from the western side up to Abdon Burf or to Nordy Bank.[2] On a clear day the view from its summit covers a wide expanse of the western side of central England and of the rugged uplands of central and southern Wales. To the south-east rise the Malvern Hills with a mistier

1 Perhaps the inexorable quarrying which has destroyed its ancient hill fort has also considerably reduced its height.
2 *See* page 40.

26

line of the Cotswolds beyond them; to the left is the Wyre Forest area and the Clent Hills, and behind them the duskier haze of the Black Country. Northwards is the rounded shape of the Wrekin, unmistakable in its lonely isolation above the miles of broad plain stretching far away into Cheshire. As you turn, the massif of the Denbighshire Berwyns comes next, a pale grey streak on the horizon, and then the sharp-peaked Breidden Hills of Montgomeryshire on the farthest limits of Shropshire. Much nearer by comparison is Wenlock Edge with the range of the Stretton hills beyond, backed by the formidable bulk of the Long Mynd, and with rolling heights receding into a far-off horizon showing the faint outlines of the crest of Cader Idris. Fringing its farther side are Radnor Forest and the Black Mountains extending across the south-west, and occasionally when the atmosphere is especially clear you have a shadowy glimpse of the Brecon Beacons in the remotest distance. Sloping away immediately below is the chequered valley of Corve Dale recalling A. E. Housman's lines,

> Wenlock Edge was umbered,
> And bright was Abdon Burf,
> And warm beneath them slumbered
> The smooth green miles of turf.

Ludlow stands out clearly because of its lofty church tower, although strangely enough from this height the town itself seems to lie in a blue hollow rather than to stand upon a hill. Following along the skyline you can see the abrupt shape of the Skyrrid Fawr near Abergavenny, and finally due south is the neighbouring Titterstone Clee with its horn-like summit thrust forward rather like a miniature Swiss Titlis.

On Titterstone there is the site of an even more extensive prehistoric hill camp covering an enormous area of nearly eighty acres. There are several ways of climbing to its summit, for example from Cleestanton up the western flank or from Callowgate on the north side; but perhaps the most popular route is by the path just beyond Clee village. Here the extensive quarrying operations are somewhat daunting at the beginning but you are well rewarded at the summit. It is difficult to believe that coal was once mined on this lofty hill; it must surely have been one of the highest coalfields in the kingdom. The cone-like crest of the hills is a ridge of hard dark volcanic rock but over the ages the stone has been cleft and shattered, and poured down the western side of the cone in a precipitous scree – a scree of great lumps of rock gigantic enough to have made excellent building material for one of the massive cyclopean walls of ancient Etruria. According to one legend this monstrous litter of scattered boulders is a relic of a battle of the giants, and there is a Giant's Chair here just as there is a Devil's Chair on the Stiperstones. Another tradition tells of a great rocking-stone which once stood among these slabs of rock, and from its name 'totterstone' the hill is supposed to derive its present name.

In ancient times when the stark outlines of the Clee hill forts with their embankments and the furrowed lines of their deep trenches stood out against the sky, it is not surprising that they aroused a sense of mystery and fear in simple country folk, and this may explain Leland's terse remark, 'Clee Hills be holy in Shropshire'. Certainly they seem to have encouraged a remarkable number of legends and superstitious beliefs which persisted right up to the beginning of this century. It was, for example, considered unlucky to put a baby into a cradle before it had been christened, and you should never rock an empty cradle, otherwise another child will occupy it. It was unlucky to throw away Christmas decorations; they should be ceremoniously burnt on the first of February, the eve of Candlemas Day, or a death would occur in the family before the following Christmas. It was also a strict rule that the horses should never be worked on the day a member of a farmer's family died. If a pregnant women saw a hare on the Clee hills she made a small tear in her dress to avoid her child being born with a hare-lip. A girl looking for a suitor would place a ladybird on her fingernail and toss it into the air as she chanted

> Ladybird, ladybird, fly away, flee,
> Tell me which way my weddin's to be,
> Uphill or downhill or towards the Brown Clee.

Her lover would come from the direction in which the insect flew away. Even the most ordinary household chores were complicated by these elaborate superstitions. No two women should light a fire together or they would be sure to fall out before the end of the day; so would any two people wiping their hands on the same towel unless they first made the sign of the cross over it. Sometimes innocent old crones suffered a campaign of persecution because they were suspected of having the baleful power of the evil eye. Even as late as 1905 Lady Gaskell's gardener firmly believed that his own brother had been 'overlooked by Becky Smout, an old gangrel body, weazen, dark as walnut juice, and the look of a vixen in her eyes. Some folks say she came to Shropshire on a broomstick some seventy years agone from Silverton on the Clee-side. 'Tis a land of witches that Clee Hill, and allus have been a stronghold of the devil.' An even more remarkable story is told which shows the type of parson who used to officiate in these parts. One of them was asked by an elderly parishioner what the reverend gentleman did for his own rheumatism. 'Do, madam? Why, I swear like hell.'

Even gipsies seemed to have had a healthy respect for the Clee district and F. H. Groome relates the experience of one who said to him,

The curiousest thing that ever happened to me was at Ditton Priors just by the Clee hills yonder. It must have been about twelve o'clock at night and we were camping in a bit of a wood with a little brook running down below. It was Lemmy here, she heard some very curious tunes right atween the tents but nigher the boys' than ourn. Just like the sound of a lot of fiddles, it was, a long way off, but wonderful clear and sweetsome, and Lemmy kicked me – leastwise so she said next morning. And the boys, they hadn't heard nought neither, but the bailiff of the fine doctor said, 'Oh, I've often heard that myself; that's the fairies'.

A round tour of the Clee Hills neighbourhood might begin at the straggling village of Caynham. A dark arched tunnel of yews and holly trees leads to the entrance of its church, and in the churchyard there is a fourteenth-century cross, headless but a splendid survival, still showing some curious figures on the four sides of its base. The red stone and the deeply splayed windows make the interior of the church rather dark, but it has a remarkable triple chancel arch with one large central lancet-shaped archway flanked by two smaller ones. It is the only one of this late Norman or Transitional date that I have ever seen. The stone vaulting of the chancel roof is a rare piece of nineteenth-century craftsmanship, and an excellent example of Victorian ecclesiastical work at its very best. North-west of the church is Caynham Camp, a double earthwork surrounded by a twenty-foot rampart. Tradition has it that during the Civil War the Parliamentarians used this ancient fortification as a ready-made base when they were laying siege to Ludlow Castle.

After leaving Caynham you turn off to the right down a narrow winding lane, passing Whitton Court, a rose-red brick Elizabethan manor house open to the public during the six months from April to September on Thursday and Sunday afternoons. The road sinks down gradually to Whitton, a secluded village with only a few houses. Its Norman church, approached by a grassy track off the road, stands isolated in this undulating upland country, sheltered by massive oaks spread round it. A squat tower and deeply splayed windows give it a rugged appearance, but as a foil to this there is an east window by Burne-Jones of exquisite delicacy. Its pure colours, especially the greens, give an overall impression of almost ethereal beauty. For its war memorial the village has a plain oak cross on a brick base, and this unpretentious tribute is strangely moving in its simplicity.

From the village we go back on our tracks for a few hundred yards, turn right at a pillar-box in the wall, and make for Hope Bagot which lies in a romantic sheltered position right under the brow of Clee Hill. The village takes its odd name from the Norman family of Bagots or Bagards who owned the small manor of Hope, and built the church that stands on rising ground over the village. It is a miniature gem of Norman work; the chevron-moulded chancel arch is neat in spite of its strength, and the diminutive altar gives an added touch of elegance to the building. An inscription records that 'this church was adorned Anno Domini 1681', and the adornment included a finely carved pulpit. On the north wall of the chancel there is a memorial with an unusual inscription recording the untimely death of a young man:

NEAR THIS TABLET
Lie the remains of what was Mortal of
BENJAMIN GILES Junr. Esq. Aged 31
Who on the 12th day of March in the year 1795
In the Prime of Life and in the Vigour of Health was
(*in consequence of a Fall from his Horse*)
snatched suddenly away from His disconsolate Parents
and from an extensive Circle of afflicted Friends by
the irresistible summons of the King of Terrors.
Reader!
Contemplate the Fate of this amiable but unfortunate
Young Man and
'Let Him that thinketh He standeth take heed lest He fall'.

On the other side of the lane opposite the church is a well still flowing with clear pure water. For centuries this was a holy well, possibly revered even in a pre-Christian era for, as Dom Ethelbert Horne has explained[1],

In the earliest times men tended to gather round natural springs of water, and they built their houses and settled down at a spot where they could most easily find one of the prime necessities of life. As pagans they would want to propitiate the god who gave

1   *Holy Wells.*

the supply lest it might fail, and they would desire to thank him for this bounty by making him offerings. In course of time the Christian missionary came upon the scene and he preached and taught at places where men had gathered – that is, round these springs of water. Then the converts would need baptism, and so a well was made use of for the purpose.

As in the case of so many other holy wells this one was regarded as especially efficacious as a cure for affections of the eyes. One reason has been suggested why this particular virtue was so commonly claimed for local wells:

As the majority of these springs owed their title of holy to the fact that it was in them the first missionaries gave the sacrament of baptism, so it was by these waters that the recipient came out of the blindness of heathenism into the light of faith. This spiritual sight was taken, as time went on, to mean sight to the eyes, and hence arose the common belief in the efficacy of the water from these wells for all complaints affecting the seeing.

From Hope Bagot we continue our way eastwards along a low wooded flank of Clee Hill, cross over the B4214 road and pass below the summit of the hill which now reveals the gashes of quarrying activities. Then we turn right at Brook Row to Coreley, a village of orchards, a few farms and a church finely situated on a shelf of high ground with wide views over the countryside. Apart from the thirteenth-century tower the church was rebuilt in the eighteenth century, and for his building material the architect chose brick, a mellow brick certainly, but contrasting oddly with the sandstone of the tower and the stone-framed pseudo-Gothic windows. Inside the building there is a tantalizing scrap of ancient glass showing the magnificent colours of a purple-robed angel with golden hair and green wings. Perhaps even more impressive is the tower arch which leans awry with the weight it has carried for over seven centuries; and in the tower chamber is a board recording that John Longmore of Clifton 'in the country of Gloucester' by his will in 1835 gave £500 to the rector and church-wardens of Coreley. The sum was 'to be invested in three per cent consols and the proceeds to be applied to the purchase of bread to be given every Sunday morning immediately after Divine Service to such poor of the parish as shall be the greatest and most deserving objects of charity, regular attendants at their parish church and also members of the Established Protestant Church of England, and to none others'. The list of rectors dates back to 1277 and begins with the name 'Simon', but other early incumbents bear more sonorous names like 'Malculine' and 'de Kynnesdelaye', and one shows his local origin as 'John Cleburie'.

As you pass over the lower flank of Clee Hill going towards Hopton Wafers you suddenly come upon an astonishing building standing in a field beside the road. Its bizarre, brick-Gothic, castellated shape is so hideous that it exercises a kind of mesmerizing fascination to which you reluctantly succumb, especially when you discover that it has a touch of poetry about it after all; for this is a water station, one of the vital links ensuring that water from the romantic Elan valley lakes, gleaming between their wild and craggy Welsh mountains, is safely piped to unlovely and unromantic baths and basins in Birmingham.

The word 'Wafers' in Hopton Wafers has nothing to do with the celebration of the mass as some would like to think, but is derived from Robert le Waffre who held the manor in the thirteenth century. It is a trim little village lying in a valley at the foot of Clee Hill, but two ugly corrugated-iron-walled cottages face the church and detract from its comely entrance. In the churchyard is a huge stone tomb, quite the largest sarcophagus I have ever seen in a village. The church was entirely rebuilt in the last century; it is an odd shape, a rectangle with rounded corners which somehow gives it the appearance of an episcopally minded Baptist chapel. One ecclesiastical novelty here is a massive marble book with the ten commandments inscribed on its open pages, but the most striking feature of the church is the excellent monument to Thomas Botfield of Hopton Court to whom the village owes the rebuilding of its church in 1825 when it was in a sadly neglected and dilapidated condition. Thomas Botfield seems to have been a great collector of lettered honours from learned societies: besides being an F.R.S. he was also F.R.I., F.H.S., F.G.S. (twice over) and M.S.A. The memorial showing him lying on a couch, his arm raised heavenwards, with his sorrowing wife beside him, is a good example of the work of that skilful Bristol-born sculptor E. H. Baily who is best known for his commanding figure of Nelson on the column in Trafalgar Square.

From the church a winding upland road goes past Hopton Court and loops back to the main road leading to Cleobury Mortimer, a small town which has managed to preserve much of its character in spite of the traffic which passes through it to and from Kidderminster and Bridgnorth. Its wide street, lined with attractive old houses and shops, and with a length of tree-lined pavement raised high above the road, curves sharply downhill past the church which thrusts a crazily warped wooden steeple to the sky. It is difficult to connect this agreeable place with one of the most arrogant and unscrupulous of the Marcher Lords, but one member of the powerful Mortimer family which gave its name to the town and owned a castle, or rather a succession of castles, in the neighbourhood was the notorious Roger de Mortimer. It was he who became the lover of Edward II's queen, Isabella, and who was later implicated in the inhuman treatment of the pitiable, deluded king when he was dragged from one stinking dungeon to another to meet at last in Berkeley Castle that igno-minious and brutal death devised with such diabolical ingenuity as the most fitting end for one who had corrupted or been corrupted by minions like Piers Gaveston.

As a corrective to this murky episode it is claimed that the fourteenth-century poet William Langland was born at Cleobury Mortimer. It is a somewhat tenuous claim, for modern scholarship more plausibly links him with a parish nearer the Malvern Hills he wrote about. A fifteenth-century manuscript states that his father was Eustace de Rokayle who held landed property near

34

Malvern. If this information about his paternity is correct, and there seems little reason to doubt it, Langland may well have been an illegitimate son born of some peasant woman living at Longland, the modern equivalent of Langland, in the parish of Colwall beside the Malverns. At all events, it is Cleobury Mortimer which has fittingly commemorated its real or adopted son with a fine east window in the church. With a brilliant show of blue, green and crimson, it depicts the sleeping figure of Piers Plowman with the Malvern Hills behind him to illustrate the opening lines of Langland's great allegorical 'epic of Christian justice', as Arthur Bryant has described it —

> In a summer season when soft was the sun,
> I dressed me in a shepherd's smock
> As though I a shepherd were,
> In the habit of a hermit, though of not holy life,
> I wandered wide about this world, wonders to see.
> In a May morning on Malvern Hills
> A strange thing befell me, a fairy vision methought,
> I was weary of wandering and went me to rest
> Under a broad bank beside a stream,
> And as I lay and leaned and looked upon the water,
> I slumbered in a sleep, so pleasantly it sounded.

One may perhaps wish that, instead of the other usual Bibilical scenes it shows, the window might have contained some of the allegorical figures described in the fierce satire of the poem. Falsehood and Truth are here, but it would have been even more interesting to see what the artist would have made of such characters as Flattery, Simony, Guile and Liar. Perhaps this would have been a challenge almost impossible to meet, and so we must be content with what has in fact been done, and done very well, in this memorial to a remarkable fourteenth-century poem. As a perfect foil to the vivid colours of the Piers Plowman window there is another east window in the north aisle with delicate pastel shades which particularly appeal to me.

35

On the floor of the chancel there is an unusual rhyming epitaph to an eighteenth-century vicar:

> The ritual stone thy son doth lay
>   O'er thy respected dust,
> Only proclaims the mournful day
>   When he a parent lost.
> Fame will convey thy virtues down
>   Through ages yet to come,
> 'Tis needless, since so well they're known,
>   To crowd them on thy tomb.
> Deep to engrave them on my heart
>   Rather demands my care,
> Ah! could I stamp in every part
>   The fair impression there.
>   In life to copy thee I'll strive,
>   And when I that resign,
> May some good-natured friend survive
>   To lay my bones by thine.

It only remains to add that the last wish was granted; some good-natured friend did survive the writer of the epitaph, and the son was buried beside his father.

The wall of the south aisle by the entrance door has an eight-eenth-century memorial which in its humble fashion is not un-worthy of comparison with Goldsmith's lines on the village school-master of sweet Auburn:

To perpetuate the memory of Mr William Brown, First Master of the Free School in this town, a truly good man, one of the best mathematicians of his time and whose mode of instruction excelled most of his contemporaries, this stone is gratefully inscribed by one of his pupils.

One bitterly cold and rainy day in April 1502 the inhabitants of Cleobury Mortimer witnessed an historic event when the funeral procession accompanying the body of young Prince Arthur from Ludlow Castle to Worcester stopped here to rest. It was a melancholy sight as the mournful cavalcade came slowly down the street, having made its weary way along the steep rough track which then crossed Clee Hill. A contemporary writer has left a vivid description of the scene:

First came the bishops and other gentlemen, then Griffin Ap Rice with the Prince's banner on a horse trapped in black; then the charre with six horses, covered with a black velvet cloth with escutcheons of gold (to be covered up with a ceared cloth in case of foul weather). All the mourners followed with hoods over their heads and noblemen by the charre and horses; also one hundred and twenty torches, all of which were put out save twenty-four when the town was past. It was the foulest, cold, wyndie and rainey daye, and the worst waye I have seene, yea, and in some places they were fain to take oxen to draw the charre, so ill was the waye.

Cleobury Mortimer's churchwardens' accounts for past centuries often throw an interesting and sometimes a curious sidelight on contemporary conditions and problems of life, as these few eighteenth-century items show:

1731 For 2 ffox heads and paid for 5 hedghogs . . 2s 3d

Foxes, hedgehogs, polecats and sparrows seem to have been very much of a pest, and they figure frequently in the books until about 1805 when they seem no longer to have been a charge on the church accounts.

1732 Edward Cropper for wine	.	.	.	£2 5s	6½d
Widow Cross for wine	.	.	.	£1 8s	1½d

If these items refer to the supply of communion wine, as they almost certainly do, the amount spent seems excessively large for a period when communion services were very infrequent, very often less than once a month. Could it be that some of the *vino sacro* was being diverted to the incumbent's personal secular use?

1732 Gave a poor travilor	.	.	.	.	8d
Oct. 11 Gave ringers upon the king's coronation			5s	od
1733 Gave to ringers for the Prince of Orange's wedding	.	.	.	.	5s od

1734	Paid for oyle and lead for paintyng the topp of the steple	2s 4d
	Gave 3 wounded seamen	1s 0d
1736	Gave a man with no tongue	1s 0d
1741	A warrant to search for the bell ropes that were stole out of the church . . .	2s 0d
1742	Ringing for the warr	5s 0d
1749	Mending the lock and cay of the steple . .	1s 0d
1755	Pd for carrying Ann Pountney from church .	6d

A very strange entry, that last one, and there must surely be a strange story behind it.

From Cleobury Mortimer we take the Ludlow road westwards as far as Angel Bank where a road to the right leads gradually off the slope of the hill down into a valley and to Bitterley, a village grossly libelled by the old saying

> Bitterley, Bitterley, under the Clee,
> Devil take me if I come to thee,

although it must be admitted that just before you enter the village there is a signpost improbably pointing to 'Bedlam'.

The church and manor hall stand cheek by jowl; in the former is a memorial which has a distant association with Shakespeare. It shows the kneeling figure of Timothy Lucy, the grandson of the Sir Thomas Lucy who, according to the old story, caught young Will Shakespeare poaching in Charlecote Park and was later caricatured for posterity in *The Merry Wives of Windsor* as Justice Shallow with 'the white louses' in his coat of arms. A memorial to John Walcot displays the three chess rooks of his coat of arms, a device granted to him by Henry V. It appears that when playing a game of chess with the king, John Walcot gave him the checkmate with the rook, and the king there and then insisted on his opponent altering the cross and fleurs de lys of his arms, and made him adopt the three rooks as souvenir of his victory over the king.

The Wrekin from Wenlock Edge.

Well at Hope Bagot.

Caynham: *Fourteenth-century churchyard cross.*

Ludlow Castle.

Much Wenlock: *The cruck house beside Saint Owen's Well.*

The Church Stretton Sheila-na-gig.

Church Stretton from Cardingmill Valley.

Acton Burnell Castle.

Pontesford Hill.

The Devil's Chair.

Old lead mine workings on the Stiperstones

Wenlock Priory: *Norman arcading of the Chapter House.*

Wenlock Priory: *Panel of the cloister lavatorium.*

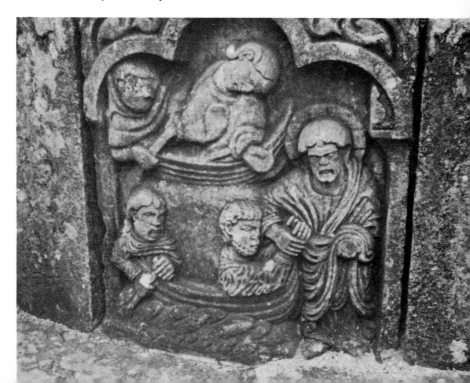

Rushbury: *Typical Shropshire domestic architecture.*

The village green at Woolstaston.

A. E. Housman's 'Hughley Steeple'.

Jacobean craftsmanship in Wentnor Church.

The River Onny near Plowden.

Gliding near the Long Mynd.

Titterstone Clee Hill.

Offa's Dyke.

'The House on Crutches' at Bishop's Castle.

Samuel Lee.

Mary Webb.

A. E. Housman.

Clun Castle.

It is recorded in the churchwardens' accounts of a neighbouring parish that in 1741 the sum of ten shillings was paid for 'whipping the doggs out of the church and keeping the people from sleeping in church during divine serviss'. The latter problem is probably still intractable, although not so publicly noticed nowadays; the former reads strangely today but was a very real nuisance in days when the altar rails were of practical use in protecting the altar from being fouled by dogs and poultry which were then allowed to wander in and out of a village church. Dogs were a hazard even as late as the mid nineteenth century as Bitterley villagers discovered one memorable Sunday morning in June. At the conclusion of the morning service, just after the blessing, a large puppy rushed into the aisle followed by a foxhound which instantly seized and bit it. He then ran out of the church and went round the house at Bitterley Court, meeting a large mastiff which had never been known to run away from any dog, but in this instance it fled, was soon overtaken and bitten. The dog then went on and found some young greyhounds, all of which he bit.

Then he went towards Mr Walcot's manservant who was coming out of church, and he bit him through his clothes. The alarm then being given of a mad dog, the congregation retiring were put in the greatest state of excitement. Unfortunately the dog went down a footpath, overtook a small boy, knocked him down and bit him badly on the shoulder. By this time the village was thoroughly alarmed; several guns were brought and the dog was shot before proceeding any farther.

Continuing by way of Cleestanton we reach the main B4364 road which passes between the two Clee heights, and arrive at the village of Cleobury North, with a church still looking just as Walter White described it a century ago, 'primitive-looking, with its rude, square, conical-roofed tower peculiar to Shropshire, reminding us of those vignettes in children's story-books of a former generation'. He also quotes the quaint epitaph inscribed on a tombstone in the churchyard:

How oft have I my Brother Sportsmen rang'd
The stubble fields, the Covers and the Plains:
My dogs and Gun, for sixty years and more,
Companions of my toil and pleasures bore
All winds and weather and oft in dead of night,
I've serv'd the best of masters, Thomas Knight;
Infirmities at length my struggling will o'ercome,
Nature bid adieu, God's blessed will be done.

From Cleobury North we take the road to Abdon which climbs
up the flank of Brown Clee and for the next few miles the road
hugs the contour of the hill high above the countryside so that
you seem to be on the promenade deck of some gigantic liner
sailing through a sea of green that ripples away to the north-east,
with the island of the Wrekin rising above it. Then as you round
the northern bluff of the hill the wave of Wenlock Edge comes
into sight, billowing like a long line of glaucous surf. Farther west
is the troubled chop of the Stretton hills, and beyond them the Long
Mynd surges darkly against the distant swell of the Welsh mountains.
There are a number of fine panoramas in Shropshire hill country;
this road I think gives the most spectacular of them all, besides
offering the climber a variety of paths up to the summit of the hill.

Instead of turning off the hillside to the village of Abdon, go
left at the telephone booth by the letter-box at Bank Farm, and
continue below the overhanging bracken-covered heights of
Abdon Burf and Nordy Bank. When you arrive at the crossroads,
continue along the lane towards Bouldon, and after about a mile
you come to one of the most appealing buildings in the whole of
Shropshire. Here, standing in a lonely field, is Heath Chapel, a
perfect example of a tiny Norman church. It is a simple, primitive
building, perhaps the work of Saxon artisans directed by a Norman
craftsman who may have been responsible for the carved arch of
the door, the only feature which is not of the simplest kind.
There is no tower, not even a belfry, and the interior is equally
humble with roughly carved pews and pulpit, crudely planed

benches, and a reader's desk with traces of the chains which once attached the Bible and prayer book to it.

We complete our journey back to Ludlow by way of Clee St Margaret and Stoke St Milborough. The former is said to have been the Roman headquarters for the fort they reconstructed on Nordy Bank. It is a picturesque village clustered around a small brook, and its church is old enough to show some Saxon work. Stoke St Milborough lies in a wooded hollow under the brow of Brown Clee and appears in Domesday Book as 'Godestock'. Presumably its name was changed to commemorate its associations with St Milburga who founded the abbey at Much Wenlock in the seventh century.[1] The ancient well bearing her name was said originally to have had a stone close by it stained with her blood; for after being pursued for two days and nights by her enemies and their bloodhounds she fell fainting from her horse at this spot.

On the opposite side of the road some men were sowing barley in a field called the Plock, and they ran to help the saint. The horse at Saint Milburga's bidding struck its hoof into the rock and at once a spring of water gushed out. 'Holy water, henceforth and for ever flow freely,' said the saint. Then stretching out her hands she commanded the barley the men had just sown to spring up, and immediately the green blades appeared. Turning to the men she told them that her pursuers were close at hand and would presently ask them 'When did the lady on the white horse pass this way?', to which they were to answer, 'When we were sowing this barley.' She then remounted her horse and bidding them prepare their sickles, for in the evening they should cut their barley, she went on her way and it came to pass as the saint had foretold. In the evening the barley was ready for the sickle and while the men were busy reaping Saint Milburga's pursuers came up and asked for news of her. The men replied that she had stayed there at the time of the sowing of that barley, and they went away baffled. But when they came to hear that the barley was sown in the morning ripened at midday, and was reaped in the evening they owned that it was in vain to fight against God.[2]

1 *See* page 45. 2 Charlotte Burne *Shropshire Folklore*.

This legend about St Milburga, the grand-daughter of King Penda, must have been eagerly listened to by many generations of village children here. Her well still flows freely, but perhaps as a sign of the times it has been enclosed in farm property – secularized, canalized and utilized.

Chapter 3

Much Wenlock and Wenlock Edge

In a short story, *Many Mansions*, Mary Webb described Much
Wenlock as a 'very Rip Van Winkle of a borough. Somewhere in
the Middle Ages it had fallen asleep and if you should wonder at
the fashion of its garments you must remember that it had not,
since the day it fell asleep, changed its coat, its hosen or its hat'.
She was in fact forestalled in her metaphor some half a century
before by Walter White who called the town Sleepy Hollow,

Sleepy is the only word that describes the aspect of the town: a
more somnolent habitation we never saw; Delft and Sierre are
brisk in comparison. For ten minutes that we stood watching in
the main street not a soul appeared, and the one that did at length
appear was an old man who paced slowly from one door to another
and forthwith left the street as vacant as before. It seemed almost
ludicrous to us that the inhabitants should think it worth while
to open their shops on any other day than market-day.

I hope the inhabitants of Much Wenlock will not take it amiss – it
is no disparagement – if I say that even today there are times when
their town still preserves this happy peace. Of course there are
also times when the unhurried passers-by in the street have to
press themselves against their ancient houses as cars and lorries
mount the pavements to pass each other, but once they have gone
by quiet falls again. The inexorable enemy time seems to be more

accommodating here, and to move more slowly; sometimes you have the sensation that you might easily do a Rip Van Winkle act in reverse, rub your eyes and find yourself transported back a couple of centuries. Not only has the town preserved something of its ancient peace; it has also managed to keep much of its impressive antiquity which you can enjoy by 'that bewitching kind of pleasure called sauntering', and so exploring in an unhurried fashion its timber-framed houses, its picturesque Guildhall, its parish church and the noble ruins of its priory. The place has a proud history, too, and a formidable number of kings have been entertained here – Henry I, Henry III, Richard II, James I and Charles I; few towns of this size could boast such a list of royal visitors. Furthermore Wenlock was formerly one of the few boroughs privileged to send members to parliament by a special charter which was granted in 1468 by King Edward IV 'at the instance of our well-beloved and faithful counsellor John Wenlock, knight, lord of Wenlock, and in consideration of the laudable and freely bestowed services our well-beloved and faithful liegemen and residents in the town of Wenlock rendered to us in our obtaining our legal right to the Crown of England'.[1]

When Much Wenlock received this charter over five centuries ago it was expressly proclaimed that it was to be in perpetuity. In 1966, however, Whitehall swept the charter aside and the borough of Wenlock disappeared under a new arrangement whereby its 22,500 acres and its population of sixteen thousand were distributed among various local authorities. But although the charter gratefully granted by Edward IV had been set aside the town was determined to celebrate the five-hundredth anniversary of the grant, and did so in 1968 with an enterprising programme of events.

In fact the story of Much Wenlock might well begin much earlier than this charter – with St Owen's Well which can still be seen a short distance away from the main street opposite the priory. St Owen was a monk who came to Wales from France in

1   L. C. Lloyd *Lord Wenlock and the Charter of 1468*.

44

the sixth century, and became a member of the monastic community on Bardsey Island off the Caernarvonshire coast. At a later period in his life he is said to have come to Much Wenlock as a missionary, and in after years the holy well bearing his name became a place of pilgrimage attracting many devout believers, among them a king's daughter, Milburga, who remained here to found a religious community. It is said that under her gentle rule the nunnery 'became like a Paradise in which the Lord had planted the fairest flowers and sweetest fruits, and amongst them all St Milburga was pre-eminent in every virtue, more especially in the grace of humility'. She was also credited with miraculous power over birds and she is generally represented standing with geese around her because she is said to have intervened on one occasion to save a neighbour's crops from the depredations of a flock of wild geese.

To her virtue and humility had been added a rare beauty which attracted many suitors. One was the son of a king and when he was rejected he determined to carry her off by force while she was visiting her lands at Stoke St Milborough. Being warned of his design she fled towards Much Wenlock, performing a couple of miracles on the way as delaying tactics. In spite of this 'when she reached the little River Corve which was there a trifling stream her pursuers were close at her heels; but she had no sooner leapt over it than the rivulet suddenly became a torrent, and put an effectual stop to the designs of her lover'.[1]

St Milburga's abbey was entirely destroyed about 874 by a force of marauding Danes, and even the site of her burial place was lost, but some 160 years later Leofric, Earl of Mercia and husband of the famous Lady Godiva, built another religious house here and this in its turn was replaced by the Cluniac priory founded by Roger de Montgomery. It was during the building of this Norman church that the lost tomb of St Milburga is supposed to have been found in circumstances related by the chronicler William of Malmesbury:

1 *See* page 41.

45

While the new church was being erected a boy running violently along the pavement broke into the hollow of the vault and the body of the virgin was discovered when a scent of balsam pervaded the whole church. She was taken up and performed so many miracles that the peoples flocked thither in great multitudes, so that broad spreading plains could scarce contain the crowds of pilgrims.

The antiquarian Thomas Fuller relates the same story, but in a more sceptical fashion:

In the reign of William the Conqueror her body (discovered by miracles wrought thereby) was taken up *sound and uncorrupted* to the admiration of the beholders; and surely had I seen the same I would have contributed my share of wondering thereunto. This I am sure of, that as good a saint, Lazarus by name, by the confession of his own sister did stink when but four days buried. Her relics enshrined at Wenlock remained there in great state till routed in the reign of King Henry the Eighth.

The 'routing' of this great English Cluniac foundation took place in 1540 when it was dissolved, meeting the same fate as other monasteries all over the country which, with the same solemn hypocrisy, were said to 'grant their houses to the king, and vest the same in him, of their own free and voluntary minds, good wills, and assents, without constraint, coaction or compulsion of any manner of persons'. Most of the members of the dissolved community seem to have remained in the district they had known and loved for so many years, and they eked out the small pension they had been granted by performing stipendiary services, or serving cures in the neighbourhood of which indeed most of them, to judge from their names, were natives. From the register notes of a contemporary vicar of the parish church we learn of the deaths of several former members of Wenlock Priory, including the organ player, 'an expert and full cunning man who did set many a sweet and solemn song to the laud of Almighty God'. There was some talk at the time of the dissolution of retaining the magnificent priory church for use as a cathedral for the county of Shropshire but the scheme came to nothing; the priory's funds were swallowed up by Henry VIII's rapacious extravagance, and the stately monastic buildings were allowed to fall into decay, a prey to weather, time and ruthless plunder.

What remains of the priory's buildings is splendid enough to make us regret all the more that such greed, neglect and ignorance have deprived later generations of what should have been a precious heritage. The church alone was of impressive proportions, over 350 feet in length; and the surviving remains of the south transept are seventy feet high. Among the most prominent features which catch the eye and stir the imagination are the three richly carved arches leading into the chapter house; the beautiful arcading on the wall of the chapter house itself; and the remains of the monks' lavatorium well-head in the cloisters with two carved panels still preserved, one of them showing a dramatic lifelike representation of Christ asleep in the boat on the lake, with four anxious figures around him. All of this is 'so exquisite as to make one grind one's teeth at the folly to which it was sacrificed'.[1]

The former prior's lodging has been happily preserved as a private house. Nikolaus Pevsner describes it as 'one of the finest examples of domestic architecture in England about the year 1500'. One of its unique features is a two-storeyed gallery on its west side, and in his *Portraits of Places* Henry James wrote of it with special enthusiasm.

A massively arched portal admits you to a beautiful ambulatory – a long stone gallery or cloister repeated in two storeys, with the interstices of its traceries now glazed but with its long, low, narrow, charming vista still perfect and picturesque – with its flags worn away by monkish sandals and with its arched doorways opening from its inner side into rooms roofed like cathedrals. Every step in such a house confronts you in one way or another with the remote past. You feast upon the pictorial, you inhale the historic. Of course there is a ghost, a grey friar who is seen in the dusky hours at the end of the passages: you are conscious of a

1   F. J. Snell *The Celtic Borderland*.

peculiar sentiment towards him which you hardly know whether to interpret as a hope or a reluctance.

It only remains to repeat that the house is a private residence, and it is not open to the public.

The monks' church was reserved for them alone; the inhabitants of the town which grew up around the priory had their own parish church. With singular and uncharacteristic ineptitude its Norman builders covered up the best part of their work – the west front – by blocking it with the tower. On the west wall of the nave is a memorial to a local doctor, William Penny Brookes, who founded the Wenlock Olympian Society. Although it was primarily the energy and persistence of a Frenchman, Baron Pierre de Coubertin, which inspired the modern revival of the international Olympic Games in 1896, Dr Brookes's own enthusiasm and work for athletics entitle him to have some share of the credit for this revival; and certainly it was largely his tireless exertions which finally led to the introduction of physical education into the schools of this country.

There are two epitaphs here which have always remained in my memory. One runs

> Here lies an old soldier whom you may applaud,
> Who fought many battles when he was abroad,
> But the strangest engagement he ever was in
> Was the conquest of self in the victory of sin.

The other records in one simple line that a youth of sixteen was

> His grandmother's friend.

There are a number of old houses in the town, some half-timbered like the Raynald's house, and some built with stones obviously filched from the priory buildings. The picturesque Guildhall beside the church is perhaps the most popular old building with visitors to Much Wenlock, especially American visitors, one of whom is reported to have offered a considerable sum for it some years ago, hoping to have it transported in sections to his homeland. The stone part of the building, nearest the church, was the old town prison, and a contemporary document states that the timber structure was 'reared' in the incredibly short space of two days. The term 'reared' is more suitable than 'built' because the wooden framework was prefabricated, so to speak. The timbers had been cut out, fitted and numbered in advance, and the frame could thus be assembled on the site and fixed by means of wooden pegs driven through the mortices. All that remained to be done was to insert the windows and fill the panels of the frame with daub and wattle – hence the surprising speed of its completion.

On one of the stout posts supporting the timber frame you can still see the iron hooks dating back to the time when it was used as a whipping-post. Formerly there was also kept here a 'scold's bridle', but this has now unfortunately – from the historical point of view, of course – disappeared. One resident of the town writing in a local paper at the end of the nineteenth century said 'I have often seen forty years ago an old woman named Judy Cookson led through the streets of Wenlock with the scold's bridle on her unruly tongue'.

The upper storey of the Guildhall contains a magnificently panelled justices' courtroom and a council chamber. Over the seat of the magistrates' bench is a Latin inscription:

HIC LOCUS ODIT,   AMAT,   PUNIT,   CONSERVAT,   HONORAT
NEQUITIAM,   PACEM,   CRIMINA,   JURA,   PROBOS

At first sight this seems something of a puzzle but the clue lies in the arrangement of the words: each noun should be read in conjunction with the verb above it:

THIS PLACE HATES WICKEDNESS, LOVES PEACE, PUNISHES CRIMES, PRESERVES THE LAWS AND HONOURS MEN OF HONESTY.

The ancient parish stocks are preserved here, and it will be noticed that they are fitted with wheels so that the unfortunate miscreant could be pushed to various parts of the town where there would be new groups of jeering spectators to greet him. A spell in the stocks was formerly one of the commonest forms of punishment, and during the period the unfortunate culprit was confined in the pillory he was often pelted by the onlookers with any kind of missile they thought most suitable for the occasion. Bad eggs and rotten fruit provided the most usual ammunition, but more dangerous things might be hurled when the crowd was in an ugly mood or the spectators bore the offender a special grudge; and it was not unknown for death to occur at times when things got out of hand. One privilege, and only one, was permitted to the victim – that of haranguing the assembled crowd, and at a time when freedom of speech was sttictly limited this was an opportunity often courageously seized by those who wished to air some grievance or draw attention to some injustice.

H. E. Forrest points out that the timbered house beside Saint Owen's Well is of more than ordinary interest on account of its age, construction and associations. It is the oldest timbered house in the town, dating probably from the middle of the fifteenth century, and it is of 'cruck' construction with the main frame of its original two storeys made in a traditional medieval fashion.

Two great boughs of oak having the same natural curve were roughly squared with an adze and set up with their feet in the earth and their tops fastened together overhead. A similar pair of timbers was set up parallel with these about sixteen feet off and a third pair the same distance beyond these. A horizontal beam joined each of these pairs to the next, forming the ridge of the roof. The spaces between these great timbers were afterwards filled by a framework of smaller timbers and this frame finally filled with 'wattle and daub'. The big pairs of timbers were called 'crucks' (i.e. crutches) and the house was said to be built on crucks. The space between one pair and the next was called a 'bay' and each bay formed one room on the ground floor and one above. When the occupier needed more room he merely added another pair of crucks at the proper distance from one end of the house, and filled in the wall-frame between, thus adding another pair of rooms to the house.

In this house the first two bays were built on crucks which are plainly to be seen on the outside of the one gable, but the third bay at the other end is framed in squares and has no curved crucks. This is of later date, probably about 1550. Another difference between the two periods and styles was that crucks were set up in the earth whereas the later frames were fastened into a square beam resting on a low foundation wall of stone a foot or so above the ground. The lower ends of the crucks in time decayed away and stones were inserted beneath them to replace the decayed portions, but in no case will any foundation wall or bottom beam be found in a cruck house. This particular house is a most interesting example as it shows both methods of construction very perfectly.

For some six years after the dissolution of the priory one of the former monks, William Corvehill by name, lived in this house which was part of his emoluments for serving as an assistant priest 'within the parish church of the Holy Trinity'. Corvehill was a Wenlock man born and bred; he seems to have become a firm friend of the vicar, and it was a happy arrangement which allowed him to remain in his home town until he died in 1546. The vicar seemed genuinely upset by his death and wrote a touchingly simple obituary about this most versatile man in his parish register:

Wm Corvehill was excellently and singularly expert in divers of the seven liberal sciences, especially in geometry, not greatly by speculation but by experience. Few or none of handicrafts but that he had a very good insight in them, as the making of organs, of a clock and chimes, and in carving, in masonry, in weaving of silk and in painting. And no instrument of music being but that he could mend it, and many good gifts the man had, and a very patient man he was, and full honest in his conversation and living. All this country had a great loss of the death of the said Wm Corvehill for he was a good bell-founder and maker of the frame for bells.

This grateful tribute to a medieval monk bridges the centuries, bringing past and present together and giving us a real sense of the richness of our heritage in local history, history which as A. L.

Rowse puts it, 'isn't something that is dead and done with but something that is alive and all around us, in our blood and bones, in our memories, in our head – if we have any head – in the things we see before our eyes'. And this sense of the living past is particularly vivid at Much Wenlock.

The ridge of Wenlock Edge stretches for nearly sixteen miles from Much Wenlock to Craven Arms following the same direction as the other Shropshire hill ranges, from north-east to south-west. Although it never rises much above 950 feet the Edge offers some magnificent views, but the first stages of the road from Much Wenlock are undeniably disappointing. For more than a mile and a half there is the desolation of limestone quarries beside the road, some of them abandoned old workings and some still in use with all the concomitant ugly nuisance of lorries scattering clouds of white dust which settles on trees and hedgerows. Marked on the ordnance survey map on the eastern side of this part of the Edge above Blakeway Farm are the words 'Major's Leap'. This refers to a limestone crag which is connected with an event in the life of Thomas Smallman of Wilderhope Manor. He was a major in the Royalist army during the Civil War, and on one occasion when he was carrying important secret despatches for the king he was pursued by a party of Roundheads. He fled over Wenlock Edge, and then seeing that escape was impossible he turned his horse aside and made for a rock on the brink of the Edge and leapt over it. The horse plunged to its death below but Major Smallwood was miraculously saved by grasping a tree growing out of the side of the rock. He slithered down almost unharmed, continued his journey on foot and delivered the precious papers without further mishap.

Once past the quarries Wenlock Edge makes ample amends by giving a superb panorama on the west side stretching over the beauty of Ape Dale to the Stretton hills, the Long Mynd and the Stiperstones, and then far beyond to the Welsh mountains rising up paler and paler as they recede into an enchanted distance. This was the view that impressed Henry James so much.

There are no waste details; everything in the landscape is something particular – has a history, has played a part, has a value to
the imagination. It is a region of hills and blue undulations and
though none of the hills is high all of them are interesting – interesting as such things are interesting in a small old country, by a kind
of exquisite modulation, something suggesting that outline and
colouring have been retouched and refined by the hand of time.
Such a landscape seems historic. The 'Edge' plunges down
suddenly and one may follow the long ridge for the space of an
afternoon's walk with a vast charming prospect before one's
eyes.

Memories of A. E. Housman's well-known lines about its
steeple will take us off the Edge down to the village of Hughley,
but when we arrive at the unassuming little place it is something
of a disillusionment to find that Housman's 'steeple' is merely a
small timber and brick bell-turret. The truth is that Housman had
already written his poem some time before he looked down on the
village from Wenlock Edge; he had even used another name for
the village in his original draft of the poem but substituted Hughley
because he realized it sounded more attractive than his first
choice. He could only deplore that this small village church was
obdurate enough not to fit in with his imaginary description of it.
He confessed that he did not foresee that in later years his readers
would find him out by making pilgrimages to the 'holy places' of
A Shropshire Lad.

Hughley need have no regrets; it is a charming village in its own
right and its church can dispense with Housman's steeple because
it has a much greater treasure in its fifteenth-century chancel
screen, extraordinarily lofty for the size of the church, and yet so
delicately proportioned that it seems to soar effortlessly and with
no suggestion of overpowering its surroundings. There is a
mysterious memorial here on the sanctuary floor, a badly worn
slab which should be protected from worse obliteration. It has the
enigmatic inscription: 'Here lyeth the body of Wm Corfil who died
by the hand of a hidden assassin. This stone is laid as a mark of

respect for the memory of a faithful and honest servant who met his untimely death in the zealous discharge of his duties.'

About eight miles beyond Major's Leap, above Upper Hill Farm, is another limestone crag with a story. It is called Ippikin's Rock and is named after an outlawed robber who lived in a cave here with a band of followers. One day when they were all inside gloating over the rich booty they had stored away, an overhanging crag crashed down, blocking the mouth of the cave and burying the robbers with their treasure for ever. Naturally Ippikin's Rock is haunted, and if you want to see the ghost you have only to stand upon it and shout

> Ippikin, Ippikin,
> Keep away with your long chin,

and immediately the robber will appear with his gold chain about his neck, and he will sweep the speaker over the rocks to his death for daring to utter the spell.

The countryside around Wenlock Edge has been well described as 'a happy landscape dotted with villages which were already old when the Conqueror's scribes entered their names in Domesday Book. Though of little note now they figure prominently in the early history of the district.' One such village worth making the detour to see is Easthope, a mile away on the south-eastern slope of the ridge. It has an Elizabethan manor house, and opposite it a cottage with the timbered end standing on crucks which have recently been strengthened with brickwork. The church was burnt out some fifty years ago and much that was valuable was destroyed, but it was rebuilt with great care and good taste. Beside the pulpit is a preacher's hour-glass in its original iron bracket which gives its date as 1662. In the churchyard under a yew tree are two raised stone tombs about which a strange story is told. You will notice that they bear a cross but no names; this is why they are reputed to be the graves of two monks who died in somewhat unholy circumstances. The two served in the kitchen of the adjoining manor house when it was a hospice belonging to Wenlock

Priory, and one night after they had been indulging in their favourite weakness, long and liberal potations, a drunken quarrel broke out between them which finally came to blows. As they struggled together they stumbled, and falling headlong down the cellar stairs they both broke their necks. In an effort to hush up the scandal the prior ordered them to be secretly buried in these nameless graves.

Continuing along the upper road over the Edge we have increasingly magnificent views not only to the west but also eastwards where there is rolling green country with Brown Clee Hill standing starkly as a backcloth. There are stopping places at several viewpoints and looking back northwards you can see the familiar shape of the Wrekin rising up from the surrounding plain. Where the road bears right and dips off the Edge to Church Stretton a lane marked 'No Through Road' and unsuitable for cars leads ultimately to Wilderhope Manor, a sixteenth-century house originally owned by the Smallman family, one member of which was the gallant soldier who figured in the incident of the 'Major's Leap'. Today the house is owned by the National Trust and leased to the Youth Hostel Association. At the time of writing it is open to the public only on Wednesdays between 2.30 and 5.30 p.m. during the six months from April to September inclusive. Situated in remote wooded surroundings the house is not easy to reach, but those who manage to visit it will be rewarded by the sight of some unusual seventeenth-century plaster ceilings, one of which has a motto also found in Easthope Manor:

DROIT DEV EST MAL MEV.

This has proved rather a puzzle to antiquarians but the riddle of the translation seems solved when it is realized that 'dev' (i.e. 'deu') and 'mev' ('meu') are the old French forms of 'dû' and 'mû' so that the sentence runs, 'Due [lawful] right is ill moved [disturbed]'.

Taking the Church Stretton road off Wenlock Edge we turn

left after a couple of miles for Rushbury along a road running below the thickly wooded crest of the Edge which rises less steeply here, its green fields sloping gently down to the fertile valley of Ape Dale. This is a countryside to be seen in springtime when there are primroses and wild daffodils to 'paint the meadows with delight'; and in early summer the bluebells take over with their haze of colour shimmering in the woodlands. Rushbury is a pleasant village of farms and with one especially attractive half-timbered manor house which retains its original form unchanged. The church is an interesting example of Early English style, the three lancet windows at the east end providing a good example of the primitive form of the transition from the rounded Norman type.

We return to the main B4371 road and turn off left to Ticklerton, continuing to Eaton along a road from which you have a view of the whole long stretch of the Edge. Eaton (or Eaton-under-Heywood, to give it its full name) is a really unspoilt, isolated Wenlock Edge village, a tiny place with less than a handful of houses, and it seems to be swallowed up by the green waves of the trees flowing down from the crest of the hill. Here of all places 'peace comes dropping slow', for here you do seem to be in a real sense out of this world. It would be worth coming a long way to see the church alone, one of the most engaging little buildings I have ever seen. You approach it by way of an archway of trees formed by yews and two great chestnuts. The site of the church is as nature made it; there is no levelling of the ground and the building simply rises up with the slope of the hill. The carved woodwork makes a splendid display, showing skilled craftsman-ship; and on no account miss the carved medieval wooden effigy lying against the north wall of the sanctuary; you are unlikely to see another like it.

From Eaton take the first lane to the left before the dismantled railway bridge and you will reach a particularly beautiful road lead-ing over the Edge by way of Westhope, and down through Siefton Batch to the B4368 road and Craven Arms. As you pass over the ridge laterally this way you see a different aspect of the beauties of Wenlock Edge. Here there are no wide vistas; but the road cuts through the rich farming land of Ape Dale and through a winding defile shady and cool in summer, alive with the songs of birds, and echoing to the ceaseless sound of streams.

On Callow Hill at the south-western end of Wenlock Edge a plain, sturdy square tower forms a conspicuous landmark, especially from Hope Dale. For those who like a climb to be short and steep a path leads up to the tower from Moorwood between Lower Dinchope and Westhope. The tower is known locally as Flounder's Folly and it bears the initials of its builder 'B.F.' and the date 1838. Benjamin Flounders was a Ludlow landowner, and according to one story he had the tower built in order to give employment to some local men during a period of depression. He also somewhat optimistically hoped that on a clear day he would be able to see from the top of his tower his ships lying at anchor in the far distant port of Liverpool. Another and perhaps more likely story is that the tower was built to mark the meeting place of neighbouring landowners' boundaries.

Close to Craven Arms, at the north end of the valley through which the River Onny flows, is Stokesay Castle, a unique example of a thirteenth-century fortified manor house. As it now exists it consists of a large rectangular building containing a great hall and a solar wing – the medieval equivalent of a drawing-room – at the south end. At the south-east angle of this is the Great Tower, sixty-six feet high and nearly forty feet across; and at the north corner is another tower with projecting timber work. The space in front on the east forms a courtyard enclosed by a wall, and entered by a beautiful Elizabethan timbered Gatehouse. The whole building is surrounded by a moat, six feet deep and with an average breadth of twenty-two feet.

The preservation of this relic of medieval England is little short of miraculous. It was garrisoned by its owner Lord Craven for the king during the Civil War and was besieged in 1645. In spite of its name the castle was never a strong fortress, but merely a fortified house, and it would have had little chance against a determined attack by the Parliamentarian forces. With commendable prudence and speed the besieged garrison surrendered after one blunt warning from the attackers that they meant business. Even more fortunate for posterity the Roundheads forebore to carry out their usual policy of destruction, and Stokesay Castle was left virtually intact apart from the removal of its curtain walls. By the beginning of the nineteenth century the buildings were no longer lived in and were so neglected that they began to fall into decay. Fortunately the castle was acquired in 1869 by the Allcroft family whose care has ensured its preservation.

For every dozen persons visiting the well-known and much photographed Stokesay Castle I suspect only about one enters the church. If true this is a pity because it contains much of interest, including a seventeenth-century gallery, a three-decker pulpit and an unusual double-canopied pew. The church was much damaged during the Civil War, and a stone in the tower arch records that the nave was rebuilt in 1654. The chancel dates from ten years later, and this in itself is something of an architectural rarity as very few churches were built at that period.

As we make the return journey along the B4368 road to Much Wenlock we pass Diddlebury or Delbury which lies off the main road to the right. The village has a most unlikely association with Mary Queen of Scots; in its church is a memorial to Thomas Baldwin, one of the custodians of that unhappy queen when she was imprisoned by Elizabeth. In some unexplained way Baldwin himself got into trouble, possibly for treating his prisoner too leniently. He was arrested and was himself imprisoned in the Tower of London where he whiled away the time by drawing on one of the walls of the Beauchamp Tower a pair of scales to represent justice; his name and the date 'Julie 1585'; and the inscription 'As vertue maketh life, so sin causeth death'. His epitaph behind the organ in the vestry is almost obliterated, but according to Hare it records his escape from 'the sea, the sword and the cruel tower'.

About a mile farther along the road at the village of Aston Munslow some 200 yards from the attractive old Swan Inn there is an interesting house which is open to the public at certain times. It is a medieval manor house which until 1946 had been the home of the same family for over 600 years, a remarkable example of the continuity of land tenure which is so often a feature of English local history. The house shows cruck construction and the later method of square timber framing. Other interesting features include inserted floors, a great hearth and chimney, an eighteenth-century hanging staircase and the remains of a Norman dovecote. In the outhouses a Country Life Museum is gradually being built up, and it is intended later to show a representative collection of both everyday and rare tools, implements and domestic articles connected with Shropshire life of generations ago.

The Crown Inn in the next village of Munslow has an ancient history dating back to the time when it was the 'Hundred House' and the meetings of the local manorial court, the Court Leet, were held here during the days of the early Norman kings. In the village church there are some unusual monuments on the north wall. The one nearest the west end is to William Churchman who died in 1602. It represents the figure of a man tied in a shroud; above and below are a skull and an hourglass. The inscription reads, 'Sonne of man, can these bones live? O Lord God, thou knowest'. Beneath are the lines,

> I in the hower of His power
> By Christ doe rise,
> And we whose bones rot under stoanes
> Our dust Heel not despise.

Another is a brass to the memory of 'Richardus Baldwin de Munsloe' who died in 1689. It was restored in 1938 by 'the Shropshire Archaeological Society as a record that Stanley Baldwin, Earl Baldwin of Bewdley, K.G., is descended from the same family'.

The other memorial, also of the late seventeenth century, shows a small shrouded figure carved in wood representing Joyce Baldwin, another member of the same family.

One native of this modest Shropshire village achieved a place in national history during the troubled years of Charles I's reign. The distinguished lawyer Edward Littleton was born here in 1589 and began his oddly erratic career with his appointment as Chief Justice of North Wales. He then proceeded to support the Parliamentary cause against the king and was partly responsible for the famous Petition of Right which presented the Commons' demand for the upholding of traditional liberties and the end of arbitrary taxation. When Charles offered him the post of Solicitor-General Littleton changed sides, espoused the royal cause, and vigorously opposed John Hampden in the notorious Ship Money dispute. As a reward the king raised him to the peerage and made him Chief Justice of England. In the following year, however, much to the king's angry bewilderment his Chief Justice sided with Parliament again, and refused to sign the proclamation declaring the rebellious Five Members to be traitors and demanding their surrender to the king. Littleton later claimed that he had taken this step to mislead Parliament as to his real intentions, and to avoid the confiscation of the Great Seal which was in his keeping; and to do him justice it must be added that he did in fact send the Great Seal to the king later, but he himself managed to avoid becoming implicated in the later collapse of the Royalist cause, and he died quietly in his bed seven years after the execution of Charles I. The historian Clarendon, his contemporary, has described Littleton as 'a handsome and proper man notorious for his courage which in his youth he had manifested with his sword'. His private life was irreproachable and he was regarded as an excellent lawyer. He was also considered an incorruptible judge, but his vacillations in politics showed that he was unsuitable to hold power in high office. By trying to be the friend of Royalists and Parliamentarians he forfeited the confidence of both parties who not unnaturally ended by doubting his integrity.

On arriving at Beambridge, instead of continuing to Much Wenlock by the less interesting main road[1] you have the choice of turning to the left into a road which will take you back to Rushbury and over the top of the Edge again by a much more striking route. Just before reaching Rushbury you pass over a bridge which once spanned a railway now removed, but the old station remains, and its conversion to a dwelling house of much character is a lesson in skilful planning. From Rushbury you return to Much Wenlock by the ridge road (B4371), and thus have another opportunity of enjoying its panoramic views from a different direction which reveals surprising variations in light and shadow.

[1] But one attraction of this road is that it goes past Shipton Hall, a handsome Elizabethan house at present open to the public on Thursdays from 2.30 to 5.30 p.m.

Chapter 4

Church Stretton and its hills

Church Stretton has been aptly described as the centre of the Shropshire Highlands; it lies in an upland valley with hills rising so steeply beside it that they give an almost mountainous character to the scenery, and yet by their fortunate north-easterly to south-westerly direction they leave the town open to sunshine. There are three separate Strettons strung along a road now mercifully relieved of main road traffic which by-passes all three places by means of the A49. Little Stretton, the most southerly of the trio, has a number of good timber-framed houses, but to see the best of the village you must walk round the loop off the main road where you will discover a stream with tiny waterfalls and a succession of miniature bridges leading to secluded cottages sheltering under the lower slopes of the Long Mynd which offer inviting walks through Ashes Valley and Small Batch. The twentieth-century black and white thatched church blends happily with the general character of the village, but its pitchpine interior shows less taste and imagination.

The Ragleth Inn here must often have been the site of performances of the open-air plays which were a popular feature of the countryside west of the Stretton hills over a century ago. The plays were all traditional, following a set pattern, and the same actors travelled from place to place, setting up their stage on two wagons outside the village inn. These were arranged so that the players as they made their exits passed into a sort of green room within the building itself where suitable refreshment for dry throats was ready to hand. There were no actresses, the women's parts being played by boys as in Shakespeare's time, and the players received no payment; instead they were generously entertained by the innkeeper who made a handsome profit from the extra customers the performances brought him. On one occasion it is recorded that as many as a thousand people flocked in from the surrounding district to witness a village performance which lasted for three hours. The proceedings began with a short prologue written in doggerel verse,

> Good morrow, gentlemen, every one,
> From half an hour to three score and ten
> We've come here to-day some pastime for to show,
> But how we shall behave indeed I do not know.

The play itself was simple knockabout stuff, childish enough to our sophisticated taste but greatly relished by an audience of simple appreciative yokels, many of whom would join in heartily with the performers when they recited certain well-known lines. At the conclusion of the play the proceedings were rounded off with an epilogue written in typical homespun verse containing a discreet advertisement for the innkeeper and some tactful flattery for the ladies in the audience:

> Our play is all over and all's at an end,
> I hope there is none of you we did offend;
> If we have offended right sorry we are,
> It was not our intention when we came here.
> We came here today for the good of the house,
> And you've well entertained us at great charge and cost;
> I hope there is each of you sixpence will spend,
> Because they are willing to make us amend.
> I pray be contented and tarry till night,
> The moon and the stars will serve you for light;
> Likewise your own sweetheart then home you will send,

And every one ought to take care of his friend.
All you men here that has a wife,
Prize her as dear as your own life,
And in your wives take your delight;
And now I wish you all good-night.

Church Stretton still has the atmosphere of an unhurried but nevertheless reasonably flourishing market town. Its High Street and its Market Place have something of a foreign appearance, rather like that of a French mountain village, especially if you are prepared to exaggerate in your imagination the height of the hills overhanging the town. There are a few old houses to be seen but for the most part the neo-black-and-white timbering here is Victorian, dating from the time when Church Stretton had a brief popularity as a spa. Yet the town has an ancient history; it was an important manor in Saxon times, and twenty years after the arrival of the Conqueror it was described as having a considerable population, a church, a priest and a mill. In Henry VIII's reign John Leland described it as 'a pretty uplandish Tounelett'; by the seventeenth century it was prosperous enough to have a spacious three-gabled, half-timbered Market House which with the typical crass insensitivity of the period was ruthlessly demolished in 1839.

The parish church is a handsome building of unusual size and dignity containing, to quote the leaflet guide, 'features which are ancient, beautiful and of interest', among them a blocked-up Norman north doorway locally known as the 'Corpse Door' as it was supposedly opened only for those bearing a coffin. Over this doorway on the outside is a crudely carved fertility figure. In most cases a Sheila-na-gig is a female figure provocatively offering herself, but here it is a debauched-looking man with arms lecherously thrust downwards and phallically suggesting the male version of the same temptation. A tiny window in the south transept is a memorial to Sarah Smith, the popular Victorian novelist who wrote under the name of 'Hesba Stretton'. The demure figure in green portrayed in the window represents the heroine of one of her best-sellers, *Jessica's First Prayer*. Another rather characterless window commemorates the town's somewhat tenuous connection with the celebrated nineteenth-century painter and sculptor, Lord Leighton, who chose Stretton as his territorial title when he was raised to the peerage.

Two epitaphs in the churchyard are worth recording. One dated 1814 is to Ann Cook,

> On a Thursday she was born; on a Thursday made a bride,
> On a Thursday her leg she broke; and on a Thursday died.

In the other epitaph a deceased husband speaks:

> Farewell, my wife and children dear
> I could no longer tarry here
> This world is frail as you may see
> Therefore prepare to follow me.
> Farewell my children dear
> Ye are in number seven
> Therefore prepare you all
> In hope to meet in Heaven.

The story is told of an American visitor who was so taken with these lines that he copied them into his notebook and on his return home sent them to his local newspaper. Unfortunately he had misread the sixth line and it appeared in print as

> Ye live at number seven.

Church Stretton is still a place of great charm and it has succeeded in preserving a certain tranquillity in defiance of the ceaseless roar and rattle of the main-road traffic near by, but even so it was with envious nostalgia that I recently read a description of the town written over a century ago when the noise on highways and byways was limited to the creaking of a farm wagon, the tattoo of horses' hooves and the jingle of harness. The description was written by Walter White when he was enjoying what in those pre-hiking days was called a walking tour. He and his companion were approaching Church Stretton from Wenlock Edge; it was a fine summer evening, a time when like most hill-girt places the town looks its best.

We were now nearing the hill range which had for some time bounded our view on looking from Wenlock Edge; steeply the rugged lane rose and fell and at length merged into a trackway on the flanks of Sharpstones and Cardington Hill. Presently we were surrounded by huge heights in whose shadow we found coolness and relief for tired feet on the soft turf, and something for observation in the rounded slopes, their steeps roughened and crested by rocks, their ferny hollows and varied patches of trees.

Twilight crept on; before we skirted his base old Caradoc had lost the gilding from his lofty brow. Then, issuing from the defile, the track hardens into a deep lane which curves down to the valley while a footpath mounts to the top of the bank. From this path we saw a spectacle of wondrous beauty. Before us rose the Long Mynd, Church Stretton lying peacefully under its sheltering height and in the deep shadow that increased the mountainous effect of the mighty hill. The amber glow still lingering in the western sky made the shadow appear the darker and the form of the massive group the more distinct; and along the wavy outlines there trembled a filmy radiance that seemed a halo hung upon the edges of the hills.

Meanwhile through the deep gulfs that separate the summits poured broad streams of light slanting down one beyond the other; golden where they rushed over the crest but reddening with the descent, until falling more and more into shadow the red deepened to purple and the purple subsided into the dusky veil that night began to draw softly over the landscape. And while we stood the dusky veil floated higher and higher; the radiant film and the streaming glory vanished; ever upward floated the veil and before we came to the town the red and the purple were lost in the sombre shadow of the mysterious hill.

The two companions found Church Stretton in a state of some excitement when they arrived in the High Street. Groups of people stood about the street talking volubly and there was a general air of expectancy everywhere.

We were at a loss for an explanation of all this until the waitress at our inn told us that 'the gas was a-going to be lighted for the first time. They had tried to light it the evening before but it wouldn't work'. It was something, we thought, to have arrived on so memorable an occasion and we watched for the great illumination. Instead of dazzling, however, there was disappointment; the gas still refused to light except at two of the lamps in which it shone with the lustre of a halfpenny candle. The gazers shook their heads doubtfully and went home to bed.

A few years later, however, according to an old guide book the gas was functioning 'with extreme efficiency and is supplied by the gasworks belonging to the proprietor of Stretton private asylum and situated at the World's End'. The writer of this *Handbook to the Capabilities, Attractions, Beauties and Scenery of Church Stretton* describes the amenities of the town in positively lyrical terms:

Here you will find peace and quietude, Alpine scenery without the discomforts of foreign travel. Here crowds are unknown, nigger minstrelsy unheard of, brass bands and barrel organs

'Like a robe pontifical
Ne'er seen but wondered at.'

Here all kinds of fresh meat, poultry, vegetables, fruit, etc., and milk can be readily obtained, and the viands are of such excellent quality; meat so prime and well-fatted; the butter, made on the spot, so sweet and delicious, eggs so fresh, milk pure and healthful; the native bacon and hams so excellently cured. Perhaps the reader may think the subject of food too much dwelt upon, but after a day's glorious ramble among the hills you will enjoy your refreshments.

One senses an even greater enthusiasm, and a more authoritative connoisseur's opinion, when the author, George R. Windsor, turns from milk to the subject of stronger beverages:

I say it with all sincerity that the nut brown ales to be had at our hostelries are worth a journey to drink, especially if you have climbed in summer heat our hills *previous to* your draught. As for adulteration – faugh! it is a thing unheard of.

67

Mr Windsor had nothing to learn from later generations about the gentle art of puffing and could even write ecstatically about the local magistrates.

No kinder-heartedmen, no truer Christian gentlemen, no higher-minded, more honourable Englishmen live than those magistrates who adorn the bench of Church Stretton Petty Sessions. It can be said without fear of contradiction that their most earnest endeavour is to do justice in all the cases brought before them. Does a person think he has a right of way through a neighbour's field, who so competent to settle the question than the magistrates? Naughty boys and girls will play truant; servants break their contracts; tramps tear up their habiliments and paupers won't work. Again their worships are appealed to. Folk will travel on the railway without the preliminary of paying for a ticket. Men must get drunk and drunken cases form a large percentage all the year round. Some men don't like to pay for their dogs; others forget the gun tax and have to interview the magistrates, generally departing purified of some of their dross. In winter there are a considerable number of offences against the game laws; people go after the timid hare and rabbit and net the plump partridge and pheasant. Bad work, better stay at home and stick to honest employment. It will wear best in the long run for we are happily favoured in Church Stretton in having a police superintendent, a gentleman much respected.

At one point in his guide book, prose fails the author and he is moved to poetical effusions of which this is a typical specimen:

> The green hills are clothed with early blossoms,
> And the bills of summer birds sing welcome as ye pass;
> Flowers fresh in hue, and many in their class
> Implore the pausing step, and with their dyes
> Dance in the soft breeze in a fairy mass;
> The sweetness of the violet's deep blue eyes,
> Kissed by the breath of heaven, seems coloured by its skies.

The popularity of Church Stretton as a holiday resort was greatly increased by the completion of the Shrewsbury and Hereford railway in the second half of the nineteenth century. A contemporary local newspaper described the excitement of this eagerly awaited event on the official opening day for this section of the line. Reading the account arouses more than a touch of nostalgia for the lively spirit of enterprise and enthusiasm which greeted the 'Railway Age', especially as the Church Stretton station which the local inhabitants were so proud of has now felt the edge of the Beeching axe, is shabbily forlorn, bereft of any staff and with only an occasional train halting furtively at its once busy platforms.

The inhabitants of Church Stretton were not behindhand in joyful demonstrations on the occasion of the opening of the Shrewsbury and Hereford railway to Ludlow. There has been from the first projection of this railway an ardent desire among all classes to see it successfully carried out. None of that gloomy foreboding respecting the injury it might do particular individuals nor the effect it might have in destroying 'vested interests' has ever been indulged in here. The inhabitants hailed with delight the opening of the line and determined to commemorate it in a way that would not easily be forgotten.

The day was ushered in by a merry peal from the bells of the old church and the celebrated brass band from Dorrington was early in attendance and added much by their admirable performance to the pleasures of the day. At 11 o'clock the whole of the inhabitants of the town and many hundreds from the surrounding neighbourhood proceeded to the station to await the arrival of the train. The railway bridge, the approaches, the platform and station were crowded with spectators; the band sent forth its enlivening strains, and above all was the glorious blue sky and the sun in splendour shining on the gay and cheerful scene. The train was welcomed by the most hearty cheering, waving of handkerchiefs and every demonstration that could testify to the good wishes of the people.

There was a tea and a dinner, and after dinner 'various rural sports in the meadow adjoining the station, such as foot-races, jongling (juggling) matches, etc., and much amusement and rollicking fun were kept up until a late hour with nothing occurring in any way to disturb the agreeableness of the evening'. The inmates of the Union workhouse were not forgotten but were supplied with a dinner of roast beef and plum pudding with a due proportion of ale, and 'sixty of the aged men and labourers in the town were plentifully supplied with bread, beef and beer. Altogether the proceedings seem to have given unmixed satisfaction, and there was none of that degrading sensuality and drunkenness which too often disgrace festivities of this kind.'

At the official dinner the first toast was proposed to the queen and the royal family; the band obliged with the national anthem. Then came a toast to the Duke of Wellington and the Army, and the band provided the 'British Grenadiers'. Then it was the turn of the Duke of Northumberland and the Royal Navy (strange that the senior service came second), and 'Rule Britannia' inevitably followed. After this there was a toast to the success of the Shrewsbury and Hereford Railway. At this the band seems to have been rather nonplussed but played safe with a popular song, 'I Love Her'. Finally came a toast to 'the health of the Directors of the Railway whose energy and determination had overcome all difficulties'. The band was now on surer ground and gave a spirited rendering of 'I Know a Bank'. After this inspired choice the dinner came to an end.

One of the great attractions of Church Stretton as a holiday centre is the variety of walks within easy reach. In addition to the Long Mynd which is described in the next chapter there is, east of the town, the straggling, rugged chain of its own Stretton or Caradoc hills which are in general highest at their south-western extremity and slope away gradually to the north-east. Their striking outlines are best seen from the Church Stretton to All Stretton road, or from the Long Mynd whose high flat moorland summit provides a striking contrast to their own somewhat ridged and angular heights.

Starting from the south the chief hills are Ragleth (1,250 feet); Hazler (1,132 feet); Helmeth (1,000 feet); and then the undisputed lord of them all, Caer Caradoc, rises to over 1,500 feet, rough and rocky on its summit, and with a long oval prehistoric camp on its crest following the contour of the hill and enclosing about six acres in its area. On the western side, lower down on the flank of the hill, is a small cavern which is popularly known as 'Caractacus's Cave' although its origin is obviously of more recent date than Roman times. Lastly, north of Caer Caradoc are the long bare humps of the Lawley which reaches 1,236 feet at its highest point.

All these hills offer excellent walks ranging from gentle climbs to steeper challenges which demand a certain amount of more strenuous effort. Each of them has its own special characteristics, different viewpoints and most convenient footpath approaches. Ragleth Hill can be climbed by way of Overdale, from a path off the top of Clive Avenue which is reached from Watling Street south of Sandford Avenue. Hazler Hill has a number of easy walks from a small road leading off Sandford Avenue, a short distance away from the town. Opposite the same road is a gated track which gives access to Helmeth Hill. Caer Caradoc is likely to be the first choice of a climber because of its commanding height, bold outline and historical interest. One popular way of climbing it is from the northern section of Watling Street by a path skirting New House Farm where there is a sign post. My own preference, however, is the somewhat more direct route by way of a signposted track from Willstone which is easily reached from Cardington.

It has already been mentioned that the road to the third and last Stretton, All Stretton, gives one of the finest views of the whole range of the Stretton hills and the pale blue cone of the Wrekin away to the north-east. According to one county historian All Stretton received its name as the results of a royal repartee.

When James the Second was travelling from Ludlow to Shrewsbury he passed through the Strettons and when he came to the first village he stopped and asked the people what was its name. 'Stretton, your majesty,' was the prompt reply. 'Stretton,' he said, 'it's a very little Stretton, I must say.' And so it got the name of

Little Stretton. He went on and arrived at a small town where they stopped to bait the horses. The king asked what was the name of this place. 'It's Stretton, sire,' was again the reply. 'Oh, I suppose it must be Church Stretton,' he said, 'as I see you have got a church here'; and Church Stretton they have called it ever since. Then the king set out again and soon came to another village and asked what the name of this one might be. 'It's Stretton, your majesty,' they said. 'Stretton!' exclaimed the king, 'Why, they are all Strettons in this part of the country.' And that is how All Stretton got its name.

Unfortunately for the authenticity of this ingenious explanation it is necessary to add that the accepted derivation of the word 'All' in the village's name is that it is a corruption of Alured, the original Saxon owner of the manor. Although it is certainly true that James did travel from Ludlow to Shrewsbury in 1687 it would have been unlikely he was in the good humour which the anecdote suggests. He had been sorely tried by a series of incidents all the way from Gloucester; at Worcester, for example, the mayor was so dull-witted and illiterate that he was quite incapable of reading or remembering a formal address of welcome to the king. It was therefore decided that the city's recorder should stand just behind him and prompt him if he happened to forget any part of the speech. When they were ushered into the royal presence and the mayor was about to begin he looked so sheepish and embarrassed that the recorder whispered into his ear, 'Hold up your head, sir, and look like a man'. Mistaking this for the beginning of his speech the mayor boldly stared the king in the face and audibly repeated, 'Hold up your head, sir, and look like a man'. The horrified recorder again whispered, 'What the devil do you mean by this?' This was likewise repeated by the flustered mayor in still more emphatic tones. The recorder then lost all patience and muttered 'By heavens, sir, you'll ruin us all!' The mayor, still taking this to be a continuation of his speech and still staring the king full in the face, repeated loudly, 'By heavens, sir, you'll ruin us all'. James was only too conscious of his unpopularity and knew only too well how little his measures were liked by most of his subjects. He started angrily to his feet at this outburst and was with some difficulty mollified even when the cause of the mayor's extraordinary remarks was explained to him.

Just before entering the village of All Stretton a small drinking fountain can be seen in the wall on the left. It dates back to the time when Stretton made claims as a spa and health resort, and there is an inscription still visible:

S. H. M. W. CO.

MANUFACTURERS OF MINERAL WATERS

THE COUND DALE SPRING

'THIS IS ONE OF THE PUREST WATERS WHICH

HAS EVER COME UNDER MY NOTICE OR OF

WHICH I HAVE SEEN ANY RECORD.' FRANCIS SUTTON, F.C.S., F.I.C.[*]

Joining the A49 we continue north for about a mile and a half to Leebotwood, a main road village with an interesting thatched seventeenth-century Pound Inn which has a dining-room partly panelled on one wall, probably the work of a skilled local craftsman. Undoubtedly the same craftsman's skill was used in making the Jacobean box pews in the church which lies off the main road in a picturesque situation high on a plateau overlooking the surrounding countryside. Although it is so near the busy traffic of the main road this is a peaceful little building with a character of its own. Apart from its wealth of woodwork in the best traditions of Shropshire craftsmanship, it also has an unusual altar containing a cupboard. Among several handsome monuments to the Corbett family is one to the memory of one member who

as one of Her Majesty's Inspectors of Poor Law was selected to organize a system of relief, first in the manufacturing districts of Lancashire and Yorkshire at the time of the cotton famine of 1863 and subsequently in London at a time of unprecedented distress in the Metropolitan Unions. Later he was appointed Chairman of two Royal Commissions to formulate schemes for taxation in the Isle of Man and Ireland.

[*] Bottling of the spring water was begun again in 1976.

This interesting historical sidelight on national taxation is followed with unintentional irony by the quotation,

They rest from their labours and their works do follow them.

It is impossible not to feel the history that is 'alive and all around us' when we turn off the main road for Longnor and Acton Burnell. Before the Normans arrived in this country there was a mill at Longnor busily grinding corn, and the thirteenth-century chapel built for the occupants of a fortified manor house is still standing here, doing faithful duty as the parish church. Longnor Hall, the gracious, seven-bayed country house built by Sir Richard Corbett in 1670 to replace the old manor house is now a country club – you may care to draw some kind of historical inference from that. The church is an unspoilt example of Early English work and it has the unusual feature of an outside stone stairway leading to the inside gallery. Of even greater interest to me, however, is one of the box pews, the last but one on the north side, which is carved with the initials R.L. and the date 1723. Richard Lee was the village carpenter who made these pews, and fifty years after he had recorded this date his great-grandson was born in the same village, and for a time followed the same trade. But young Samuel Lee from an early age had a passionate love of book learning, a vigorous independence, a capacity for hard work and a natural linguistic talent which he had to develop unaided. His life is a remarkable story of genius which refuses to be hampered by lowly origins and limited opportunities; his parents were only humble working folk of Longnor like his great-grand-father, and their boy was educated at the village school until he was twelve years of age, when because of his obvious intelligence he was sent away from the village to be apprenticed to a Shrews-bury carpenter to follow the family trade in the county town. He earned six shillings a week, much of which he spent on secondhand books, for he read avidly and no sooner had he absorbed a book than he would sell it back to the shop and buy another in its place.

74

One of the books contained quotations in Latin; this was a challenge to his restless curiosity and he immediately set about learning the language from an old Latin grammar he picked up at the bookstall. Latin led him on to Greek, and then an interest in biblical studies made him learn Hebrew. From now on the study of languages was an all-absorbing passion and it is said that by the time he was twenty-five he had mastered the elements of Chaldee, Syriac, Samaritan, Persian and Hindustani.

Meanwhile he had married at an early age, had a family of three children and continued to maintain himself by his work as a master carpenter. Then fate stepped in; his expensive and indispensable collection of tools was lost or stolen and he suddenly made up his mind to follow a new way of life. For a time he taught in a Shrewsbury school and gave private lessons in the then somewhat esoteric languages, Persian and Hindustani. It was about this time that he sent 'an autobiographical letter with twenty specimens of his calligraphy in different oriental scripts' to the Church Missionary Society. Unfortunately this letter has disappeared from the Society's archives but the Committee was obviously impressed because a few months later they made him a grant of £150 to go to Queens' College, Cambridge; an unexpected windfall, as he had been hoping merely to be sent by the Society as a missionary to India.

At Cambridge in addition to his own academic work he performed a number of useful services for the C.M.S. At their request he completed a Syriac New Testament and wrote *Prayers from the Liturgy in Persian*. The Society realized his value as a linguist and in 1814 he was allowed to bring his wife and family to live in the new C.M.S. House in Salisbury Square. He was given a gratuity of fifty pounds and became known as 'the Society's Orientalist'. Among other assignments he translated into Hindustani *Little Henry and His Bearer*, a moral tale written by the wife of an East India Company man, and that Company gave him a gratuity of one hundred guineas. He also designed a new kind of 'fount of Persian types on rhomboidal bodies'.

In spite of all these extra-mural activities Lee obtained a brilliant degree and then took holy orders. At the end of his student career he had mastered no less than eighteen languages, and later he was appointed Professor of Arabic at Cambridge. Afterwards he was Regius Professor of Hebrew there for seventeen years, but in later life he moved to the west country, was a canon of Bristol Cathedral and vicar of Banwell in Somerset. At the time of his death he had achieved the status of an internationally famous figure in the realm of linguistic scholarship, and his obituary notice paid tribute to his self-reliance and unfaltering confidence in his own abilities – 'we believe Professor Lee to be the most astounding living instance of successful self-education; of great powers of mind contending with vast difficulties, fortifying themselves with substantial and most extensive learning and progressively rising from obscurity to the first rank of the literary world'.

The road from Longnor to Acton Burnell follows the track of the old Roman highway which led to Viroconium and which must have been trodden by countless legionaries and citizens making their way to the busy Roman city in the shadow of the strange shape of the Wrekin which now looms against the skyline beyond the River Severn. Acton Burnell, too, must be peopled by ghosts of the past, for it was here that Robert Burnell, Bishop of Bath and Wells, and Edward I's chancellor and friend, entertained his royal master. When twilight falls and shadows close round the ruined walls of the castle beside the church, it does not need much imagination to see the ghostly forms of the stalwart king, the proud courtiers, and the graceful ladies rakishly eyed by the genial, shrewd and worldly chancellor himself. Although in theory a celibate bishop he had contrived to father a whole brood of bastard children and at the same time to keep his see. The pope protested in vain; the king, although his own private life was of unblemished virtue, was prepared to overlook even such openly scandalous behaviour in a chancellor of such charm and of such brilliant administrative ability.

Robert Burnell was an enterprising and enlightened builder; he was responsible for the Great Hall of the episcopal palace at Wells, and at Acton Burnell he built the church in addition to the so-called 'castle', which was really a fortified family home the chancellor was granted a licence to build and crenellate in 1284. The ruins are impressive and show that it must have been a tall rectangular building, some eighty feet by sixty, with embattled towers at the corners. The king was entertained in the village a year before the granting of the licence and it is suggested that the two gable-ends east of the castle are all that remains of Burnell's original house. It was a building of unusual length, at least 160 feet, and although it is popularly known as the 'barn', the original structure may very well have been the residential hall where Edward I stayed. Perhaps it was later relegated to use as a storage barn when the fortified castle was completed. It must also have been the meeting place of the parliament which issued the Statute of Acton Burnell, regulating the processes by which merchants could prove and collect debts owing to them. It has often been said that this was the first parliament in which representatives of the Commons took part in the deliberations by legal royal authority, but it must be remembered that representatives of the chartered boroughs had also been summoned to Simon de Montfort's parliament some eighteen years before.

The size and dignity of the church are unusual for such a small village and reflect the interest, rich patronage, care and money lavished on it by Robert Burnell who was determined to make it worthy of the place where his family had lived since the twelfth century. Perhaps the north transept will be of greatest interest on a first visit. In its north-east corner there is a table-tomb surmounted by a remarkably fine monumental brass depicting the armoured figure of Sir Nicholas Burnell, a beautiful example of fourteenth-century craftsmanship. When I was last in the church two young students were taking a rubbing of it and I was given a detailed description of this fascinating method of making a copy of ancient brasses. One of the students had been an enthusiastic devotee of this hobby for some time, and although he had copied dozens of brasses in various parts of the country he considered this one of the finest he had ever seen. 'You've only got to look at the lifelike expression on his face', was his comment. I surmised from this particular interest of his that he must be reading history or some kindred subject, and I expressed some surprise when I learnt that he was in fact taking a degree in chemistry. 'You see,' he explained, 'you've got to keep a sense of balance and have other interests besides science. Anyway *I've* got to; otherwise I might start thinking that science was the be-all and end-all of living.'

There are two other stately monuments in the north transept. The ornate sixteenth-century memorial to Richard Lee stands well over twelve feet high and has two life-size effigies of him and his wife with their three sons and nine daughters. Beside him lies one of his gauntlets out of which peers what was obviously a pet of the family, a diminutive dog of the toy breed so popular at that period. On the opposite wall is a fine memorial to Sir Humphrey Lee of the same family showing him with his wife and six 'weepers'. The monument is the work of Nicholas Stone, a well-known seventeenth-century sculptor and architect who was official Master Mason to both James I and Charles I. According to contemporary records it was designed, made and set up at the cost of just under sixty-seven pounds.

Perhaps it is because in childhood days stories of Roundheads and Cavaliers capture our imagination so strongly that the figure of the Puritan is one of the best known in English history. Indeed it has been said that any intelligent child can describe or draw you a picture of a Puritan as well as he can describe a nursery Noah's ark. Countless narrative pictures like *When Did You Last See Your Father?* have made us familiar with the supposedly typical Puritan figure – red-nosed, sharp-featured, Bible in hand; with broad-brimmed hat, wide collar, sombre-coloured coat; and bearing some outlandish, adopted, biblical-sounding name like Macaulay's Sergeant Obadia-Bind-Their-Kings-In-Chains-and-Their-Nobles-With-Links-of-Iron. And there is an equally clear picture of the Puritan's wife with her striped petticoat, apron, bunched-up skirt, deep linen collar, and white cap with perhaps a hint of side curls acting as a foil to the sly twinkle in the eye revealing that behind the demure exterior there was still that irrepressible feminine coquetry which not even a Cromwell could crush. But these are merely imaginary pictures; two miles south of Acton Burnell is something real – a tiny chapel where you can see the interior of a Puritan church just as it was in the seventeenth century.

Langley Chapel is a few hundred yards along a side-turning off the road to Cardington. You enter by putting a sixpence into the slotted lock, and then you are inside a building both unique and beautiful. There was a chapel here in the Middle Ages serving the nearby Langley Hall whose gate-house and length of embattled wall still remain beside the farmhouse farther along the lane. When the Hall disappeared and the local population dwindled there was no longer any need for a place of worship here, and by the first half of the nineteenth century the building was abandoned and neglected. Paradoxically it was this neglect which saved the original features; if the building had continued in use the restoring zeal of the later years of that century would undoubtedly have swept them away. In 1915 the building passed into the care of the Ministry of Public Buildings and Works, and the superlative fittings and furnishings have been carefully preserved. The result is that in this humble building, surrounded by lonely fields and within the long wooded slope of Wenlock Edge, you can now enjoy the comely charm of the unspoilt interior of a seventeenth-century Puritan church which actually has the date 1601 recorded on one of the collars of its roof. There are beautifully carved high box pews for the gentry and tenant farmers, and behind them roughly hewn benches for their labourers and servants. In accordance with the custom of the Puritans the communion table, set well away from the wall, was originally provided with benches on three sides of which only two remain. In view of the fact that Puritans did not usually kneel at the 'Lord's Table' it is surprising that the benches are provided with kneeling-rests. Perhaps they are later additions, or could it be that the Lord of the Manor was of 'advanced views' and insisted on them?

You will notice that the elaborate reading desk has a double seat and that the pulpit is movable. There are few places I know that have more 'atmosphere' than this chapel, and it is not difficult to re-create in one's imagination a typical Sunday meeting here, the seats all occupied by solemn-faced men and women and their children, all listening, or perhaps pretending to listen, to the long denunciatory sermon or the bleak dissertation on Foxe's *Book of Martyrs* pronounced by a lugubrious minister. The dedication of Langley Chapel, like that of Heath, is unknown, no record of it having apparently been preserved. This anonymity although curious is not unique; it is said that out of some fourteen thousand Anglican churches in England something like five hundred ancient ones appear to have no dedication because their names have been forgotten through disuse, and not even the usual sources of information – ecclesiastical documents, testamentary directions in old wills, etc. – have revealed them.[1]

The deep-set lane to Cardington continues through the hamlet of Ruckley where a notice formerly warned 'Rough Cobble Road.' This thirty yards of paving stones might well have been the remains of a Roman road, but according to ancient Shropshire folklore it was part of the Devil's Causeway miraculously laid down in one single night; and

if you cross the causeway at midnight you will meet the devil

1 At the time of writing the chapel is closed until further notice owing to the theft of a valuable piece of furnishing, but the Ministry hopes to make arrangements for its future opening when suitable security precautions can be taken.

himself in the shape of a black man with cow's horns and hoofs, riding on a white horse. There is no danger in the meeting for anyone with a good conscience going on a lawful errand. The devil passes by all such persons like a flash of light. But if any man is going on a bad errand or has lived a careless godless life the devil will set upon him and struggle with him and leave him half dead.[1]

Just beyond the cobblestones at the lowest part of the valley the road passes over a miniature bridge about three feet high, with an arched opening for the brook it spans. The arch is of roughly hewn blocks of sandstone and is obviously of the same age as the paved section of the road. Farther along to the left is a spring which has never been known to dry up even in the driest summer. It is locally known as Frog's Well from another old tradition that the devil and his henchmen haunt it in the guise of frogs. Roman Bath, its other name, suggests that it dates back to Roman times, a supposition just about as trustworthy as the explanation of Frog's Well. The lane has now been resurfaced.

Past the Devil's Causeway I prefer to go to Cardington by taking the lane marked to Church Preen and then turning almost immediately to Plaish.[2] You pass through a succession of deep winding lanes more Devonian than many Devon lanes and at intervals quite overhung by trees. In high summer the air is heavy with the scent of flowers, and the banks are a blaze of colour with foxgloves, willowherb, loosestrife, dog roses, meadowsweet, cow parsley, vetch, meadow cranesbill, honeysuckle, blackberry blossom, the glowing bronze of young hawthorn leaves, the dark cool green of ferns and the pale blue of that daintiest of all wild flowers, the harebell. Another attraction of this way is that you can get a glimpse of Plaish Hall which Nikolaus Pevsner has described as the most important house of its date in Shropshire. The greater part of it was built by Sir William Leighton, Chief Justice of North Wales and one of the Council of the Marches during the reign of Elizabeth I. The house is not open to the public

1 Charlotte Burne *Shropshire Folklore*.
2 The name is sometimes spelt 'Plashe'.

and the most impressive feature to catch the eye of the passer-by is the remarkable collection of brick chimneys, those 'gloriously overdecorated chimneystacks of the early Tudor age'.[1] An unlikely story of their origin is sometimes told which redounds, unfairly I am sure, to the discredit of the worthy Justice. It is said that while this new house of his was being built he sentenced a master builder to death for some proved felony, and then discovered that he was a renowned craftsman in brickwork. The Justice suspended the sentence and challenged him to build a set of chimneys for Plaish Hall which no other builder could possibly imitate. The wretched prisoner, hoping to obtain a pardon, worked feverishly to produce a masterpiece and indeed surpassed himself, but in spite of his success the judge allowed justice to take its course and the builder was hanged after the completion of his work.

In spite of the serenity of its appearance Plaish Hall seems, according to tradition, to have had its troubled times in the past. On one tragic night a murder was committed in one of the bedrooms, and the consequent splashes of blood on the door were said to reappear again and again however many times the door was repainted. It is impossible not to be reminded of Oscar Wilde's *The Canterville Ghost*, and to wonder if the tell-tale marks were eventually removed by the application of 'Pinkerton's Champion Stain Remover and Paragon Detergent'. Another story concerns a party of clergymen who for some unexplained reason were assembled in the house one Sunday night, playing cards when presumably they should have been at evensong.

All the doors were locked when suddenly they were burst open without any apparent cause. The men locked them again but presently they burst open a second time and again a third. Then the Old Nick himself appeared in the midst of the company and they all rose up and fled except the host whom the others basely left face to face with the enemy. None ever saw that wretched man again either alive or dead.

1   Nikolaus Pevsner *Shropshire*.

You can see a lifelike effigy of Chief Justice Leighton in Cardington church. He lies rather uncomfortably on his side, an imposing figure in an elaborate tomb with his wife and the kneeling figures of two sons and five daughters – one of them having died as a babe is shown in swaddling clothes leaning against a skull. The epitaph may be fulsome by modern standards but somehow it has a ring of sincerity often absent from others of the same period.

HERE LIETH THE BODY OF WILLM LEYGHTON OF PLASHE ESQ CHEIFE JUSTICE OF NORTH WALES AND ONE OF THE COUNCIL IN THE MARCHES OF WALES WHICH PLACES HE EXERCISED BY THE SPACE OF ABOVE FORTIE YEARS WITH GREATE SINCERITIE AND WITHOUT COMPLAINT. HE WAS HUMBLE IN PROSPERITIE IN HOSPITALITIE LIBERALL, TO THE POORE BOUNTIFULL, LOVINGE TO HIS FAMILIE, AND TO HIS FRIENDS, TENNANTS AND NEIGHBOURS COMFORTABLE, AND TO ALL CURTEOUS AND AFFABLE. HE WAS CONTENTED WITH THE COMPETENCE WHEREWITH GOD BLESSED HIM SUFFICIENTLY FOR HIS CALLING.

It is difficult to believe that a man given such a tribute could really be guilty of the shabby trick attributed to him by tradition and could have so heartlessly used a condemned mason to build his now famous chimneys; but there may still be some sceptics ready to quote Byron's cynical lines,

> As soon
> Seek roses in December – ice in June
> Hope constancy in wind, or corn in chaff;
> As believe a woman or an epitaph . . .

One other epitaph in the church never fails to please me by its simplicity and by the sudden surprise of its blunt conclusion. Artistically engraved on copper and fixed to the north wall of the chancel it commemorates Thomas Norris who died in 1753 at the age of fifty-eight. He was

A pious Christian, True Englishman, Affectionate Husband, Sincere Friend and Good Neighbour. An Example Worthy to be Coppyed.

From Cardington take the lane to Stoneacton and Wall Bank which drops down to the B4371 road. You turn right and then after a few yards go left to Ticklerton for Acton Scott where our tour of the Church Stretton area comes to an end. The sixteenth-century Hall at Acton Scott was built by the Acton family who also owned the house at Aldenham Park near Morville. One member of this ancient Shropshire family was Sir John Acton whose strange adventurous life was linked with some of the stirring events of the Napoleonic wars. After a noteworthy career in the navy Acton entered the service of Ferdinand IV, king of Naples. He proved a diligent administrator and successfully carried out a complete reorganization of the Neapolitan navy. His ability earned him rapid promotion, and he became in quick succession generalissimo, minister of finance and prime minister. His favour with the king and his powerful influence at court not unnaturally aroused jealousy and intrigue against him, but Acton was shrewd enough to maintain his position of power. One particularly bitter rival was despatched to London as Neapolitan ambassador, and when he suddenly died shortly afterwards there was an ugly unfounded rumour that he had in fact been assassinated by secret agents on Acton's orders.

When the French invaded Italy in 1793 Acton fled with the king and queen to Sicily, but he later resumed office when Ferdinand was restored to power. The virtual reign of terror which was now instituted by Acton led to his ultimate downfall, and in 1806 he was exiled to Palermo with the royal family. Six years before at the age of sixty-four he had obtained a papal dispensation to marry his seventeen-year-old niece. Their son, named Ferdinand after the Neapolitan monarch, was the father of the historian Lord Acton who is alleged to have refused to touch any of his grandfather's fortune because he regarded the money as 'tainted' – a gesture which would certainly be in keeping with the character of one who had a reputation for the scrupulous honesty of his scholarship and the probity of his personal life.

Chapter 5

The Long Mynd

Few of us, even if we wished to, can experience the mysterious fascination which grips the mountaineer as he grapples with the difficulties and dangers of towering heights but those of us who nevertheless have the urge to climb or even just to walk up steep paths to a summit; to feel we are above the restless noise and movement of main roads; and to have the joy of watching changing lights and colours, at their best when seen from high places, can still go to hills which exercise the same attraction. For, after all, it is only a question of relativity in size and height. Stevenson pointed out long ago that 'even greatness can be found on a small scale; the mind and eye measure differently. Bold rocks near at hand are more inspiring than distant Alps'.

This longing for hill country is something innate in many people and is felt by many more than admit it. Many years ago I read some lines by an unknown writer which vividly recapture the sudden tug of this passionate desire,

> I want to stride to the hills! My feet cry out
> For hills! Oh, I am sick to death of streets;
> The nausea of pavements and people always about;
> The savagery of mortar and steel that beats
> Me under, hedges me in; the iron shiver
> Of traffic: I want to stride to the hills, I want

85

Hills toned frantic silver on a quiver
Of scarlet; hills that hunger and grow gaunt!

When I lived in Switzerland I discovered that the special characteristics and moods of particular mountains, expected and accepted by those familiar with them, are also sensed even by strangers. Less lofty English hills, too, have their own atmosphere and peculiarities which are if anything accentuated by their smaller scale. For example, the special quality of Somerset's Quantock Hills is their unruffled serenity so well suggested by the soft rich curves of their contours, and so different from the harsher olive green slopes of the Mendips, or the stark dramatic outline of the historic Malverns.

The bulky stretch of the Long Mynd[1] is not Shropshire's highest hill but it is certainly its most massive, with its broad moorland summit covered with heather and whinberries, some ten miles in length, from three to four miles broad, and nearly 1,700 feet in height. An ancient track, the Portway, runs along much of its summit, studded along its course with a succession of prehistoric barrows. On the north-west the range falls away rather steeply and on the south-eastern side it is cleft by a number of deeply cut valleys known as 'batches'. Many of these offer attractive walks and one of them, Cardingmill Valley, is a well-known beauty spot leading to the Light Spout Waterfall and to the summit of the hill. Like many other mountains of much greater height the Long Mynd is not to be trifled with in stormy winter weather when thick mists can blot out familiar landmarks with disconcerting suddenness. A century ago, when the present roads were barely discernible tracks, hazards of this kind might be much more dangerous, as Thomas Wright recalled in his book *Ludlow Sketches*:

The range can be a wild and dangerous district in the worst kind of weather and not only have many lost themselves but some

1 The adjective takes the stress and 'Mynd' rhymes with 'tinned'.

have actually perished in it. People remember many fearful hunting accidents which have happened through fog and snow storms coming on suddenly. A very fine horse was thus lost not long ago just above the Cardingmill Valley. A fog blew up suddenly and the rider who was going to meet the hounds missed his way and soon found that he was in danger. He slipped from his horse just in time to save his own life, for a moment afterwards his horse rolled down the precipitous bank and was found afterwards dashed to pieces on the rocks near the stream. A farmer met with a similar misfortune still more recently but unfortunately he could not disengage himself quickly from the saddle and he rolled over with his horse and both were crushed together. Thus we need not wonder at finding places along the hills which bear such names as 'Dead Man's Hollow' and 'Dead Man's Beach'. The last fair of the year held at Church Stretton used to be popularly distinguished by the significant name of 'Dead Man's Fair' on account, it is said, of the number of men who after attending this fair have perished in the attempt to return home over the hills in the dark nights of early winter.

H. W. Timperley considered that the Long Mynd looks most impressive when viewed from under Helmeth Hill:

. . . the valleys, batches and hollows show their opening steeps between shoulders and then are hidden like secret ways to the hill's innermost places. That is what they are, with precipitous sides terraced by sheep tracks and dotted here and there with weather-twisted thorns and sometimes broken by the outcropping of dark-toned rocks. The shoulders reach back to join each other round the heads of the hollows and merge with the great backbone of the hill which is not a sharp ridge but a narrow upland weathered into gently undulating smoothness at an altitude which makes heather and bracken, many kinds of lichen and moss, and a thin-bladed mountain turf its natural covering. Wind and weather keep the top bare of trees. I like to see it under Helmeth because of the contrast between the pastoral greenness of the valley against the more sombre greens and browns and greys – conifer plantations under slopes of turf and bracken leading up to heather and whin-berry – that stain rather than brighten the Long Mynd when seen at a distance; and because of another contrast which puts the settled ease of the valley, the life of its little fields against the wild spirit of the hill and, when I remember the burial mounds on the top, makes me wonder what the people who placed them by the ancient track thought of the Long Mynd.

An exploration of the Long Mynd and its neighbourhood might begin at Church Stretton, through All Stretton and then by way of the road to the left just before the railway bridge and the join-up with the A49. This leads us to the northern slopes of the Long Mynd itself, and to Woolstaston with its miniature village green and a church mysteriously figuring in thirteenth-century records as having been 'a sanctuary for felons'. There is some well-carved woodwork here which was the work of a local carpenter and is connected with a remarkable story of courage and endurance. A former rector of this village had agreed to look after the church at Ratlinghope on the western side of the Long Mynd when owing to various circumstances it was without a parson. This undertaking necessitated making a journey of four miles over the hills and consequently E. Donald Carr altered the time of his second service at Woolstaston from three o'clock to six so that he could take an earlier afternoon service at Ratlinghope.

It was a pleasant enough ride in fine weather but he soon found it was no easy task in winter when there was a risk of mists and the tracks were so slippery with frost or snow that he was forced to make the journey on foot. In spite of all the difficulties, in summer and winter, in sunshine and in rain, for more than eight years he crossed over the hill every Sunday with unfailing regularity and prided himself on never missing a service. Then came one terrible Sunday on 29th January 1865, when a heavy fall of snow had covered the hills and made him wonder if he should attempt the journey. After a little hesitation he made up his mind not to disappoint Ratlinghope's congregation and set off earlier than usual. He arrived with some difficulty, conducted the service and then set off over the hill for home. The almost incredible story of his experience is vividly told by himself in *A Night in the Snow or A Struggle for Life*.

It was with considerable difficulty that I made my way up the hill as I had to walk in the teeth of a violent gale. The force of the wind was most extraordinary; I have been in many furious gales but never in anything to compare with this as it took me off my legs and blew me flat down upon the ground over and over again. The sleet too was most painful, stinging my face and causing so much injury to my eyes that it was impossible to lift up my head. However I continued to fight my way through it and at last reached the crest of the hill. Though I could not see many yards in any direction I knew at the time exactly where I was as I passed the carcase of a mountain pony which I had noticed earlier on the way to Ratlinghope.

A further struggle brought him to another landmark which he recognized and after a short rest he started again hoping to come to a fir plantation after which he thought he would have no difficulty in finding his way home. Then he realized with a sudden sense of real fear that he had lost his bearings:

Having been blown down again and again I had probably in rising to my feet altered my direction unconsciously. It was moreover now becoming very dark. After a while I became aware that the ground under my feet was of a wrong shape, sloping downwards when it should have been level and I then knew that I had missed my way. Suddenly my feet flew from under me and I found myself shooting at a fearful pace down the side of one of the steep ravines I had imagined lay far away on my right. I thought to check myself by putting my stick behind me, but I came into contact with something which jerked it out of my hand and turned me round so that I continued my tremendous glissade head downwards lying on my back.

At last by using one leg as a hook he succeeded in getting himself the right way up and having extricated himself from the snowdrift at the bottom of the ravine he climbed with difficulty up the opposite bank, sometimes with snow up to his knees, and more often up to his waist. Having arrived at the top he walked some distance along the crest and then,

. . . suddenly again I lost my footing and shot down the hill as far as I can judge on the opposite side into another ravine. This was, if possible, a more fearful glissade than my previous one; it was a very precipitous place and I was whirled round and round in my descent, sometimes head first, sometimes feet first, and again sideways, rolling over and over until at last by clutching at the gorse bushes and digging my feet into the snow as before I once more managed to check my wild career and bring myself to a stand, but I had lost my hat and a pair of warm fur gloves which I had put on over a pair of old dog skins. The loss of these fur gloves proved very serious to me as my hands soon began to get so numbed with the cold that they were comparatively useless.

Struggling in this manner the lost man passed the whole night in the snow and when at last morning came it brought with it a thick mist. Faint with hunger and beginning to feel the effects of both snow blindness and his frost-bitten hands he began to fall down more and more frequently. At last he heard the sound of water; it was from the Light Spout Waterfall. He floundered on through the snow and when he seemed to have reached the utmost degree of exhaustion he heard voices. He called out, stumbled and as he sank to the ground a party of cottagers who lived in Cardingmill Valley came towards him. They lifted him and supported him as he limped back to one of their cottages. After resting a while he was taken to Church Stretton where even his closest friends scarcely recognized him, 'dressed in borrowed clothes, exceedingly thin, with bloodshot eyes and fingers stiff and swollen, the middle finger more resembling a dead stick than the living member of a human body'. The miracle was that he had survived at all, for during the horror of that journey he had been struggling uninterruptedly for twenty-two hours. As he himself said it was this continual activity which saved him –

I trust that no one who may chance to read these pages will ever have to undergo my experience, but if they do I hope that the

90

remembrance of my adventure will occur to them; for surely it teaches as plainly as anything can that even in the most adverse circumstances no one need ever despair; and shows how an individual of no unusual physical powers may, by God's help, resist the overwhelming temptation to sleep which is usually so fatal to those who are lost in the snow.

His book *A Night in the Snow* sold so well that its proceeds provided the pulpit, reading desk, lectern and altar rails which are such an interesting feature of the church. On the north wall a tablet commemorates the Rev. Edmund Donald Carr's connection with the parish, 'for forty-five years in sole charge, thirty-six years as rector', but there appears to be no record here of that fearsome night on the Long Mynd in the blizzard.

From Woolstaston the road climbs steadily up to the tumuli which have the odd name of Robin Hood's Butts, odd because no known tradition connects the legendary outlaw with Shropshire. Perhaps the name arises out of a popular confusion with a real personage, Wild Humphrey Kynaston, the younger son of a good family who was outlawed for murder at the end of the fourteenth century. He earned a reputation as 'the ideal outlaw who robbed the rich to give to the poor, who took off the leader from a team of three horses and hooked it on in front of a cart drawn by a single one; who asked for a drink at a neighbouring hall, tossed off the ale at a draught and rode away with the silver cup in his pocket; whose every want was supplied by the rich who feared him and by the poor who loved him'.[1]

You are now on the broad crest of the Long Mynd and can walk to your heart's content over miles of paths through heather and thickly growing bushes of whinberries, those delicious little bluish-black berries which grow in several parts of the country under the various names of whortleberries, bilberries or blaeberries. There was a time when the whinberry season provided a welcome extra income for poor families living in the district. E. Donald

1 Charlotte Burne *Shropshire Folklore.*

Carr records that fruit up to the weight of five hundred pounds used to be gathered on Long Mynd in a single season and he described the busy scene as he witnessed it a century ago:

To the poor people for miles around the whinberry picking is the great event of the year. The whole family betake themselves to the hill with the early morning carrying with them the provisions for the day; and not infrequently a kettle to prepare tea forms part of their heavy load. I know no more picturesque sight than that presented by the summit of the Long Mynd towards four o'clock on an August afternoon when the numerous fires are lit among the heather and as many kettles steaming away on top of them, while noisy chattering groups of women and children are clustered around, glad to rest after a hard day's work.

This wide expanse of lofty moorland is still wild and inhospitable at heart. I have walked over it many times and even in summer when the sky is clear and the air heavy and motionless with heat there seems to be something grudging about the hill's veneer of toleration for those who walk here. On grey winter days when a piercingly cold wind whistles about you, rustling shrilly in the dead bracken and dry heather, you can sense something more hostile in this bleak desolation, and it is not difficult to imagine the ruthlessness of the snowstorm E. Donald Carr battled against.

The road signposted to Ratlinghope[1] dips down steeply to the valley on the west and gives some notable views of the Stiperstones especially at sunset when their weird rocky outcrops stand out bleakly against the coloured sky. The village of Ratlinghope is remote, hidden in a fold of an elevated valley, and from the road there is a glimpse of the simple church from which E. Donald Carr set off on his perilous journey through the storm on that fateful Sunday over a century ago. At Bridges close by there is a Youth Hostel, the Hugh Gibbins Memorial Hostel, which makes a convenient centre for young walkers and climbers in the district.

Wentnor, a breezy upland village, is perched high up on a

[1] Pronounced 'Ratchup' rhyming with 'Catch up'.

shoulder of one of the lower ridges of the Long Mynd. On the east side of its churchyard the well-known 'Hurricane Stone' commemorates an unusual local tragedy.

One Sunday morn 'Bout Nine a'Clock as we Lay in our Bed,
By Hurricane of Wind and Snow all three were killed dead,
The House and we were Blown away as many well did know,
And for that day could not be found all for the depth of snow;
Fourteen poor souls were under it, but with us were killed seven,
I hope the Lord hath Pardoned us and Received our souls in
    Heaven.

To see a really isolated Long Mynd village you should make the short journey up a side lane to Myndtown which stands on a knoll right under the frowning height of the hill. A tiny church, a farmhouse, a rectory and wide views over the valley of the River Onny – this is the sum of Myndtown and it should be enough to make the detour worth while.

At its southern point the Long Mynd comes to an end somewhat abruptly at Plowden where the River Onny and the road run between the last steep slopes of the hills and Plowden Woods. In this neighbourhood are two great country houses with historic associations. Walcot is a large red brick house more remarkable for its beautiful setting than for any grace of style. It was built for one of Shropshire's most famous sons, Robert Clive, the founder of the former British empire in India. Clive's early years were marked by the turbulence and independence of his spirit. In Macaulay's time the old people of the neighbourhood still remembered having heard from their parents

how Bob Clive climbed to the top of the lofty steeple of Market Drayton and with what terror the inhabitants saw him seated on a stone spout near the summit. They also relate how he formed all the idle lads of the town into a kind of predatory army and compelled the shopkeeprs to submit to a tribute of apples and halfpence in consideration of which he guaranteed the security of their windows. He was sent from school to school, making very little progress in his learning and gaining for himself everywhere the character of an exceedingly naughty boy.

How the naughty boy to the great relief of his parents was packed off to India 'to make a fortune or die of a fever at Madras'; how he twice attempted to commit suicide and the failure of the loaded pistol to fire convinced him that he was intended by Providence for something great; and how he became the hero of Plassey and a great if controversial figure in national affairs is now all part of English history. This house built for him after his final return to England is more closely connected, not with his glory but with the last clouded years of his life when in spite of the acknowledged 'great and meritorious services he had rendered to the state' and his proved talents as a brilliant soldier, a wise ruler and a just administrator, he was regarded by many of his countrymen as an unscrupulous, perfidious and cruel tyrant who had undoubtedly accepted vast sums from native princes even if he had not been bribed by them. No comfortable country seat like Walcot, no fortune or honours could dispel the melancholy which clouded his mind. His long residence in India had affected his health and to alleviate his physical suffering he had resort to opium. He became a slave to the habit and in a sudden fit of depression this great soldier and statesman died by his own hand at the age of forty-nine.

The other famous house in the neighbourhood is Plowden Hall dating mostly from Elizabethan times. It is a picturesque timbered building with no such melancholy associations, although it does have a number of the secret hiding-places which are regarded as *de rigueur* in any house belonging to an ancient Roman Catholic family. One famous member of the family was the sixteenth-century lawyer Edmund Plowden who is popularly supposed to have given us the old phrase 'the case is altered, quoth Plowden'. One version of its origin relates that the lawyer was approached by a client who wanted to know what legal remedy was available in the case of a herd of swine trespassing on the plaintiff's land.

'There is of course a very good remedy in the law of trespass.' began the lawyer and was immediately interrupted by the client. 'But, you see, these are your own animals.' 'Ah,' said Plowden shrewdly, 'then the case is altered.'

This story hardly fits in with the character of a lawyer who was regarded by his contemporaries as one who 'in the integrity of his life was second to no man in his profession', and a more likely explanation is that Plowden, himself of course a Roman Catholic, was defending another of that faith who was standing trial for hearing mass. The lawyer managed to elicit from the evidence that the service had in fact been conducted by a layman masquerading as a priest so that informers could report on those who were present. Immediately the astute lawyer seized upon the point and exclaimed, 'The case is altered; no priest, no mass' and his client was acquitted.

Two centuries after Edmund Plowden's time the family had as their chaplain a Jesuit priest whose life story reads more like a novel of improbable adventures than a recital of sober facts. Thomas Falkner was born in 1707 and strictly brought up as a Presbyterian. After being educated at Manchester Grammar School he qualified as a doctor and later joined the crew of a slave ship belonging to the South Sea Company as a ship's surgeon. During the voyage he fell dangerously ill and was put ashore at Buenos Aires. Here he was tended with such skill and devotion by the Jesuits that on his recovery he resolved to show his gratitude by becoming a Roman Catholic. After a period of time he was admitted to the Society of Jesus and for nearly forty years was one of their most energetic missionaries among the wild native tribes of South America whose respect and affection he won by his zeal, humanity and skill in medicine. When the growing unpopularity of the Jesuits drove them from South America Father Falkner gave up his strange nomadic life and returned to England. After acting as chaplain to Roman Catholic families in various parts of the country he finally settled at Plowden Hall where he died in 1784.

It has been suggested that Plowden Hall is the original of the house described in the introductory chapter of one of the earliest of the nineteenth-century mystical 'problem novels'. J. H. Short-house's *John Inglesant* tells the story of a young seventeenth-century Englishman torn between the conflicting claims of Roman Catholicism and Protestantism. The book opens with a description of the house in

that part of Shropshire which partakes somewhat of the mountain characteristics of Wales combined with the more cultivated beauties of English rural scenery. The ranges of hills, some of which are lofty and precipitous, which intersect the country, form wide and fertile valleys which are watered by pleasant streams. The wide pastures are bordered by extensive plantations covering the more gradual ascents, and forming long lines above the level summits. It was an old and very picturesque house, jumbled together with the additions of many centuries, from the round tower-like staircase with an extinguisher turret, to a handsome addition of two or three years ago. Close by was the mutilated tower of a ruined priory, the chancel of which is used as the parish church. A handsome stone wing of one storey, built in the early Gothic style, and not long completed, formed the entrance hall and dining-room, with a wide staircase at the back.

Although Shropshire is specifically mentioned some readers consider that the description of the house more closely fits Little Malvern Court in Worcestershire which is alongside a ruined priory still used as the parish church.

In the north transept of the church at nearby Lydbury North there is still a Plowden Chapel built by Roger Plowden as a thank-offering for his safe return from imprisonment during the Siege of Acre at the time of the Crusades. It is a dank empty place and its general appearance of sepulchral gloom is heightened by the sombre iron railings around a tomb which are said to have been used as a supporting hearse for the coffin before it was lowered into the vault below. It is a relief to emerge from the forlorn atmosphere of this deserted ghostly chapel and to enter the sunny brightness of the Walcot Chapel in the south transept and to see some craftsmanship which in spite of its age is still vitally alive – the artistically written creed and commandments which were set up over the screen three hundred years ago.

The return to Church Stretton can be made by one of the most spectacular routes in the whole of the Shropshire hill country.[1] From the A489 at Plowden a lane branches off north at an acute angle to Asterton and runs along a high shelf right below the steep side of the hills and with open views westwards of the distant hills and valleys. You see Myndtown on the left isolated on its small mound like an islet in a sea of green, and in the far distance the line of the Stiperstones is etched against the sky. Beneath you and ahead are the rough quaggy fields of Prolley Moor which in old Shropshire legend was said to be the sleeping ground of crows, and the place where witches held midnight revels. As late as the beginning of this century according to Lady Gaskell's book *Spring in a Shropshire Abbey* old folk in the district would recite these traditional lines to their grandchildren,

> Dead 'orse, dead 'orse,
> Where? Where?
> Prolley Moor, Prolley Moor.
> We'll come, we'll come,
> There's naught but bones.

At Asterton another lane signposted 'Gliding Field' rises sharply up the hillside and leads to the summit. It is a tough gradient, one in four, but there are few bends and you are soon rewarded by some breathtaking views from the top of the Long Mynd. Southwards the crest of the hill stretches away in a wide undulating line until it sinks down in grassy billows towards Plowden. To the west a medley of hills forms a background for Prolley Moor and Wentnor, and as a sombre background to the whole scene there is the harsh outline of the Stiperstones. It is an unforgettable experience to see this landscape on one of those

1 *See* Chapter 2 for its possible rival.

blustery days when clouds scud across the sky and the sun gleams and fades in sudden spurts so that patches of the hills and valleys alternately light up and then fade away as the dark shadows chase swiftly over the countryside.

The road passes by the 'Soaring Ground' of the Midland Gliding Club which although established only some thirty years ago is one of the oldest of its kind in the country. Its founder was the late Charles Espin Hardwick who in the early thirties was determined to find a suitable site in the Midlands which could be used by a gliding club for local enthusiasts. It was only after a long search that a site on the Long Mynd was chosen as fulfilling the essential requirements of 'a long, flat, gently sloping area for elementary training, and a steep long hill ridge facing into the allegedly prevailing westerly winds for soaring by advanced pilots'.

Even after the choice of a site the club ran into many difficulties including a number of legal disputes over land and boundary questions, but finally on Boxing Day 1934 fifteen flying members and six non-flying members gathered on the summit of the Long Mynd for the inaugural flying meeting and the club was launched – to a literally flying start. The full story of the club's activities, its trials and triumphs, up to the outbreak of the war is told by Air Commodore L. P. Moore in *A Synoptic History of the Midland Gliding Club*. In this short history he also gives a fascinating description of a 'glider's eye view' of the southern Shropshire hill country after he had been catapulted off the Long Mynd in a glider.

I now headed freely beneath a sheet of billowy clouds north-westwards towards the crags of the Devil's Chair loosely perched upon the Stiperstones.

The wide lush valley to my half-left thrust westwards between Linley Hill and Hopesay Hill to the ancient little market town of Bishop's Castle and to the Clun Forest. It was one of those days when only the earth's curvature limited one's distant vision, and beyond the rolling ranges of the Shropshire highlands and of Wales, stood clear as crystal against the blue sky the noble contours of Plynlimon, Cader Idris and Snowdonia. With a little imagination one could easily believe that one could just see the sea of Cardigan Bay.

We were just over the Stiperstones on the same heading. Just beyond and below, derelict Roman lead mines littered the valley floor. To the left Corndon Hill in rugged isolation while straight ahead Stapeley Hill and beyond the Long Mountain and King Offa's Dyke stood between us and the Welsh mountains.

It was soon time to return to base. Heading eastwards the Long Mynd now lay across our path like a huge elongated kite, some ten miles in length, pointing its tail towards the south-west. Its further side was as serrated by deep shady batches between smooth arched fingers as it was sharply defined on its nether flank – at least along its southern half, whence the nature of the mountain was seen to change from one of wild bilberry and heather and new forest to a more diffuse tableland having a measure of cultivation. The historic Portway could easily be traced from where it climbed up at the village of Woolstaston, to traverse in a near-straight line the spine of the mountain, until descending sharply at its southern tip to Plowden.

If that first vision of the western rampart of the Long Mynd had been to the eyes of this glider pilot too good to be true, then the same could be boasted for the panorama they had dwelt upon from above that mountainous summit. The former immediately answered the question as to why Espin Hardwick and his pioneers had decided after first acquaintance to establish the Midland Gliding Club on the Long Mynd and why they had worked so strenuously in those early days to secure its future on the mountain. The latter surely represents the just reward for their labour and enterprise.

It may be added that the club today flourishes as never before and has a membership of 182 flying members and fifty-one non-flying members.

The road continues along the broad high moorland of heather and whinberry bushes by the route of the ancient Portway until at Boiling Well it meets another road coming up from the western side between Bridges and Ratlinghope which offers another striking alternative way of travelling over the hill. We take the road to the right for Church Stretton which after a time plunges down abruptly past the Devil's Mouth and then giddily skirts the very edge of the deep Cardingmill Valley with a vertiginous precipitous drop beside the steeply falling road. A sumptuous panorama is spread out to the north-east which can be enjoyed even without the soaring wings of a glider – outliers of the Long Mynd and the furrowed prehistoric camp aslant the edge of Bodbury Hill; farther east the sinewy shapes of the Stretton hills with the unmistakable humps of Caer Caradoc and the long undulating crest of the Lawley standing out clearly. On a clear day you can see the Wrekin beyond, aloof and seeming to tower over the plain spread around it. Due east there is the long green line of Wenlock Edge and behind it the solemn twin-peaked height of Brown Clee Hill oddly dwarfed by the distance. At last the road drops less steeply, the sides of Cardingmill Valley seem less dizzily overhanging and we arrive at Church Stretton, the starting point of this round tour of the Long Mynd and its neighbourhood.

Chapter 6

The Stiperstones

The British geologist Murchison considered that there is no more singular feature in the physical geography of England than the Stiperstones, that long dark ridge over 1,700 feet high, with its stark shapes of broken and serrated ledges of rock jutting skywards to form the summit of the range and 'standing out on the crest of the hill like rugged cyclopean ruins, some of the principal of which are fifty to sixty feet high and from one hundred and twenty to one hundred and thirty in width'. At close quarters the range is equally impressive, showing the ravages of centuries of wild winter weather which has lashed it with rain and hail, wind and snow, finally toppling over some of the great crags and splintering them into the thousands of smaller rocks and stones littering the slopes. It is hardly surprising that these harsh surroundings and their brooding atmosphere of mystery should breed such legends as that of Wild Edric.[1]

The highest of the series of rocks is named the Devil's Chair because according to one story the Devil made his way from Ireland with an apron full of stones to fill up Hell Gutter (Shropshire for ravine) on the side of the hill, and he sat down here to rest. When he got up his apron string broke and all his stones were scattered around the Devil's Chair where they remain to this day.

1 *See* page 5.

Another story relates that of all countries in the world the devil hates England most. If the Stiperstones sink into the earth England will perish, so whenever the devil has nothing better, or worse, to do he comes and flings himself down in his chair in the hope that his weight will sink the hill.

Perhaps the most interesting approach to the Stiperstones is from the north end, by the Shrewsbury road (A488) to Pontesbury (pronounced as if spelt 'Pontsbury') where Mary Webb and her husband came to live after they had spent the first two years of their married life at Weston-super-Mare in Somerset.[1] The chief landmark here is the isolated, strongly humped Pontesford Hill (Pontesford is pronounced with three syllables) which rises abruptly and crouches beside the village like a watchful lion. Its top is split into the two summits of Pontesford Hill itself and Earl's Hill, each with an entrenched camp, double-banked and with a ditch. They may be of British origin and are generally thought to be connected with the battle fought here in the seventh century between the West Saxons and the Mercians, and recorded in the Anglo-Saxon Chronicle: 'In this year 661 Kenwealh King of Wessex fought at Easter at Posentesbyrig, and Wulfhere son of Penda (of Mercia) laid the country waste.' From both the summits there is a splendid view; westwards up the valley of the Rea Brook to Montgomery in Wales; northwards to the towers of Shrewsbury and over the Shropshire plain undulating with an occasional low hill; and southwards are the nearer and loftier Shropshire hills, the Long Mynd and the Stiperstones.

Pontesford Hill was formerly the scene of a picturesque custom. Every year on Palm Sunday crowds of people used to climb to the summit to look for the Golden Arrow, and a regular 'wake' or merrymaking was carried on there, with games and dancing and drinking. The mysterious Golden Arrow had been supposedly dropped by a king or a fairy, or in a battle (as it was variously reported) on the hill many centuries ago, and would only be

1   *See* page 130.

recovered by the destined heir to an estate, or by the maiden seventh daughter of a seventh son searching for it at midnight; but on its discovery some great estate would be restored to the true heir or some unknown spell would be removed.

From Pontesford we take the road to Habberley, a remote little place with an attractive seventeenth-century house opposite the church. Habberley was the home of William Mytton, the eighteenth-century local historian who was connected with a family famous in the county for centuries. Another member of the same family was a notorious figure engaged in much less innocent pursuits than writing the history of Shropshire. This John Mytton, 'mad Jack' as he was known to his contemporaries, was lucky or unlucky enough to inherit a large fortune in 1798 when he was two years old. Within the space of a few years he contrived to get himself expelled from two schools, and had violently assaulted the unfortunate private tutor who had been ill-advised enough to undertake his further education.

After attaining his majority and coming into his inheritance he entered parliament and represented Shrewsbury for one year, but he found a more suitable outlet for his great physical strength, his taste for crazy acts of bravado and his love of rough practical jokes, in hunting, shooting and gambling. In his *Memoirs of the Life of John Mytton* 'Nimrod' has related some of the reckless exploits of this unbalanced and not particularly prepossessing Regency country squire. On one occasion he rode full speed across the treacherous holes of a rabbit warren 'to see if the horse would fall', and when it did fall – heavily – rolling over on its rider, he had his usual good luck and got up unshaken and unscathed. A crony of his challenged him with a large bet to drive a double-horsed carriage across country at night. Mad Jack accepted at once and set off at a gallop through the darkness over a deep broad drain, surmounted a fence thirty-seven yards wide, and then successfully negotiated two thickly planted quickset hedges. On another occasion in winter he stripped stark naked and swam across an icy pond with his gun so as to get a better shot at some wildfowl.

Nor were his escapades confined to outdoor pursuits. One riotous night in Shrewsbury he smuggled two foxes into the bar of the Lion Hotel and chased them around the room until the bottles and glasses lay in shattered heaps on the floor. To fortify himself against any ill-effects from these eccentricities he consumed a ration of between four and six bottles of port wine every day. He would generally begin his potations in the morning while shaving, and once when drinking his first glass he was attacked by a violent fit of hiccoughing which he immediately tried to frighten away by setting fire to his own nightshirt. He was said to be fond of his children; if he was he had a curious way of showing it, for he would toss them high in the air as if they were lap-dogs in spite of their howls of terror. When they were mere babes he was in the habit of screaming hunting 'view-halloos' close to their ears and was particularly addicted to throwing oranges at their heads. If anyone remonstrated he would retort, 'Pooh, it's nothing when they are used to it'.

It is scarcely surprising that after a few years of this reckless way of life he had run through his fortune; his estate at Halston was sold up; and he was imprisoned for debt in the King's Bench prison where he died of *delirium tremens* at the age of thirty-eight. It was admitted that John Mytton by his folly 'had destroyed a time-honoured family and a noble estate, the inheritance of five hundred years', yet such is the attraction of a dashing character, good humour, high spirits and openhandedness that even the most brutal of mad Jack's practical jokes were condoned, and the great crowd present at his funeral proved that already he had become something of a legend as a popular 'sportsman'.

From Habberley you turn down the road signposted 'Bridges' and go along a lonely but beautiful country lane. Take the right hand road at the first fork, and then left where there is a cattle-grid. The lane passes between hills, and then there is a sudden glimpse of the first rocky crags on the northern ridge of the Stiperstones, looming harsh and inscrutable even in summer sunshine. On a grey day the mysterious shapes of the jagged outcrops rise up aloof, eerie, and with more than a hint of malevolence. The range figures as the Diafol Mountain in Mary Webb's first novel *The Golden Arrow*, and she describes with accuracy and the insight of a poet the appearance of this 'long mammoth-like shape' and its Devil's Chair.

On the highest point of the bare opposite ridge now curtained in driving storm-cloud, towered in gigantic aloofness a mass of quartzite, blackened and hardened by uncountable ages. In the plain this pile of rock and the rise on which it stood above the rest of the hill-tops would have constituted a hill in itself. The scattered rocks, the ragged holly-brakes on the lower slopes were like carved lions beside the black marble steps of a stupendous throne. Nothing ever altered its look. Dawn quickened over it in pearl and emerald; summer sent the armies of heather to its very foot; snow rested there as doves nest in cliffs. It remained inviolable, taciturn, evil. It glowered darkly on the dawn; it came through the snow like jagged bones through flesh; before its hardness even the venturesome cranberries were discouraged. For miles around, in the plains, the valleys, the mountain dwellings, it was feared. It drew the thunder, people said. Storms broke round it suddenly out of a clear sky; it seemed almost as if it created storm. No one cared to cross the range near it after dark – when the black grouse laughed and the cry of a passing curlew shivered like broken glass. The sheep that inhabited these hills would, so the shepherds said, cluster suddenly and stampede for no reason, if they had grazed too near it in the night.

The lane continues along a shelf of the hills below the main ridge, and then before reaching Bridges you turn right at a sharp hairpin bend by a farm on a corner, and you approach the Stiperstones along their flank. If you are driving you can park the car here, climb to the ridge and walk the length of the range in both directions, north and south – to the Devil's Chair and to the other craggy masses each of which has a name, like Scattered Rock,

Cranberry Rock and Nipstone Rock. If your visit coincides with the whinberry harvest season you may be tempted from walking by the rich flavour and large size of the fruit here; and even without walking you can enjoy overlooking an historic landscape on the borderland of this once turbulent Marchland where the mountains of Wales roll westwards far into a distance which shows its real glory at sunset, in a flood of scarlet and gold fading to a solemn olive green, and then to the enveloping dusky purple of approaching nightfall.

The road continues over the crest of the Stiperstones and then drops down to old mining country which makes up in historic interest for what it lacks in beauty. Nearly two thousand years ago the Romans were mining for lead here, and during the last century some attempts were made to revive mining operations in the district, notably at Snail Beach, Vassons, Grit Mine and Potter's Pit. Walter White, walking here in 1860, was not much impressed by the operations which 'hardly compared with those of Durham and Northumberland, either in their mechanical appliances or in the energy of the labour'. In one newly opened mine in which a potentially profitable vein of lead ore had been struck, 'the operation seemed to be like playing at mining; there were two boys breaking the ore and one man washing it with a sieve in a tub of water'. It was a stiflingly hot day and climbing down from Nipstone Rock he found an odd conveyance called a cider-cart which was

a wagon containing half a dozen barrels of cider, one of which was tapped and placed peeping out at the tail, convenient for drawing. The woman to whom it belonged had drawn up under the shadow of a shed, and so, availing myself of the same screen I sat down and took a pint of cider. On the opposite side of the road a number of miners lounged in the sunshine enjoying the idleness of pay-day and calling now and then for 'Another pint, missus!' Perhaps hard cider at fourpence a quart is not one of those drinks which 'never fails to kittle up our notion', for they appeared none the happier nor was their talk any the livelier for their potations. The woman told me that she brewed forty hogsheads of cider every year and came up out of Herefordshire to find customers along the road. It was hardish work travelling in the hills; but the miners always lightened the load.

We continue along a winding road to Pennerley under the brow of the hill which seems especially high here as it rises sheer from the side of the road. A number of places along the way bear the unlikely name of 'Beach' – Perkin's Beach, Mytton's Beach and Snail's Beach; the word is a derivation or corruption of 'batch', meaning an open space or ground situated near a river. Old lead-mining operations are much in evidence, especially at Crowsnest where there is a strange mine-shaft building, and at Snail's Beach where great grey heaps of slag glimmer like ghosts. But 'Nature is creeping up slowly'; there are trees to cover the ravages of the miner; acres of wild broom make a brave show in spring; and carefully tended flower gardens blossom beside the houses.

This interesting road joins the A488 just before Minsterley where the sign of the Bath Arms recalls a link with the great house of Longleat in Wiltshire, for Sir John Thynne, the builder of that mansion, was also the owner of the gabled Hall in this village. Another member of the same family, William Thynne, was a Clerk in Henry VIII's household but has earned a more important place in history as the first editor and publisher of Chaucer's collected works for which he deserves the gratitude of every student of the poet.

Minsterley church, built in the seventeenth century, is a fascinating building looking for all the world as if it had been made in Holland and dropped out of a toy-box on to its present site. It has round-headed, stone-framed windows set in the brickwork of the building, and its wooden belfry looks oddly foreign. Hanging above the west gallery are a number of maidens' funeral garlands. These interesting survivals of an ancient custom are about a foot in height and consist of a wooden framework covered with linen to which are attached lilies and roses made of pink and white paper. Hanging from the frame are short blue and white paper streamers, and inside is a pair of white paper gloves. In former days these maiden garlands were laid on the coffin of any young girls who died before their wedding day; they were the 'virgin crants' which the churlish priest in *Hamlet* begrudged Ophelia:

> Her death was doubtful,
> And, but that great command o'ersways the order,
> She should in ground unsanctified have lodg'd
> Till the last trumpet; for charitable prayers,
> Shards, flints and pebbles should be thrown on her;
> Yet here she is allowed her virgin crants,
> Her maiden strewments, and the bringing home
> Of bell and burial.

Very few of these maidens' garlands have survived; to have kept seven of them at Minsterley since the eighteenth century is a remarkable achievement, and it was a wise precaution to cover them with polythene so that these relics of the past may long be preserved for posterity.

Chapter 7

The district of Clun Forest

The Clun district in the south-western extremity of Shropshire has been well described as 'that remote outlying cantle wedged in between the Welsh mountains of Montgomeryshire and Radnorshire'. Its hills consist not so much of a range as a succession of rounded heights split up by valleys and then merging into the wild open moorland of Clun Forest which in places rises up as high as 1,600 feet to meet the mountains spilling over the border. In early Norman days this inaccessible region of the Marchland became virtually semi-independent, especially as its overlords had been granted any land they could wrest from the wild Welshmen; and the delimitation of the boundary between the two countries was not finally settled until the reign of Henry VIII. Clun itself was included in Montgomeryshire until 1537 when it became part of Shropshire. Even today there are parts of the region which seem to be only officially English; the speech is no longer Salopian but more akin to the lilting Welsh. Even some of the buildings look Welsh: 'those prim, grey, sober-fronted dwellings of Clun, for example, look just as if they had slipped across from the other side of the border.' A study of the place names in the region will reveal the extent and limits of the Saxon settlements; often Offa's Dyke shows the line of demarcation where English names like Mainstone, Churchtown and Weston give way to the Celtic names of Bettws-y-crwyn, Bryn Mawr and Cwm Ffrydd.

In the sixteenth century Leland wrote that the 'faire Forest of Clunne is a great forest of red deer and roes'; it extended over many thousands of acres and although parts of it were well wooded some of it must have been the rough lofty moorland it is today. There is a common confusion about the real meaning of the ancient term 'forest' which only in a popular and comparatively modern sense signifies a great tract of trees. Originally it was an unenclosed district over which the king strictly reserved to himself all hunting rights, and maintained special forest courts to administer laws to protect these rights. The 'forest' may have included extensive woodland but its essential feature was that it was 'privileged for wild beasts and fowls to rest and abide in, in the safe protection of the king for his princely delight and pleasure'.

There is abundant proof, however, that the ancient Forest of Clun, covering some 17,000 acres, was originally well wooded and that even in Elizabeth's reign a considerable number of trees still remained; but over the centuries building requirements encroached steadily on the forests of the Shropshire hills. The wealth and splendour of the timbered houses throughout the district show how heavily woodland so conveniently to hand must have been depleted, and the charcoal burners' activities must have added still more to the wholesale depredation of the forests. Although the first conifer planting in Shropshire (one of the earliest in the whole country) took place at Linley Hall as long ago as the end of the eighteenth century when European larch was grown, and although the Powis family began some extensive planting of conifers at Walcot Hall from the first half of last century, a planned re-afforestation scheme is of comparatively recent date and is the result of the activities of the Forestry Commission and of private owners, many of whom now develop their woodland according to plans approved by the Commissioners. As a fair proportion of their Shropshire plantations is in the Clun district this is a suitable point at which to examine in greater detail the work of the Forestry Commission over the whole area.

In Shropshire hill country the Commissioners control six areas – part of Kerry Forest; part of Mortimer Forest; Walcot Forest; part of Long Forest; Stiperstones Forest (formerly called Habberley Forest); and part of Haughmond Forest. These cover an area of nearly 8,500 acres of which nearly 7,500 acres have already been planted. The species used vary with the types of soil and the differences in climatic conditions. In Kerry Forest, for example, and on the higher hills, it is mostly Sitka spruce; on drier, stony soils Scots pine is used, and in the deeper soils of Mortimer and Walcot Forests the Douglas fir and both European and Japanese larch do well. Norway spruce is more suitable for the heavier soils while in Long Forest on the limestone slopes of Wenlock Edge a considerable amount of the hard woods – oak, beech and sycamore – has been planted, mixed with larch or western red cedar. There is a sharp rainfall gradient from the Welsh borderland down to Craven Arms and there are local increases at Church Stretton and the Clee Hills. These variations have had a considerable influence on the distribution of Sitka spruce and Japanese larch both of which prefer a rainfall of more than forty inches.

The 'conifer revolution' in afforestation took place in a great part of this area during the past century and the process was still further extended in the nineteen-twenties, thirties and fifties. Broad-leaved species need rich soils and sheltered sites in order to make first quality timber and as these requirements are limited in this area (except in places already given over to agriculture) the planting of broad-leaved varieties has been less than five per cent of the total. Yet small areas of the original broad-leaved forest, mostly oak, which formerly covered much of this land have been retained and they provide a welcome variety of forest scenery and a more suitable environment for certain kinds of wild life. On the larger private estates broad-leaved varieties have always been used more extensively, partly because on the whole the soils of these estates are better than those of the hill areas planted by the Forestry Commission, and partly because it was the deliberate policy of these landowners to preserve a typical English woodland landscape for aesthetic and sporting reasons. Yet even on private estates the harsh economic facts of life have encouraged an increasing use of conifers since the last war – after all, soft wood means hard currency.

Quite a strong body of opinion opposes extensive conifer afforestation and criticizes the Forestry Commission's predilection for softwoods. These opponents of large-scale planting of conifers point out that they radically and irredeemably alter the special character of an English landscape. In reply the Forestry Commissioners can justly claim the important contribution their commercial afforestation can make towards the rural economy in areas of steep-sided, unfarmable and otherwise unproductive areas of hill country.

Although by virtue of its geographical position and its historical associations the town of Clun is the capital of this district we shall approach it by way of Bishop's Castle, half town, half village, which climbs up a southward sloping hill, gently at first and then with a sudden steep spurt towards the site of the now vanished castle. The town was originally known as Lydbury Castle; its change of name occurred when the manor was given to the Bishop of Hereford. The reason for this transfer is linked with a typical story of love and treachery in Saxon times when King Ethelbert of East Anglia fell in love with Alfreda the daughter of the Mercian King Offa who built the dyke. The father approved of the match but his queen was jealous and determined to kill her daughter's suitor. She invited him to her room where a seat had been specially prepared for him over a trapdoor. When he fell helplessly into the pit below, her guards stabbed him to death. The murdered king was buried in Hereford Cathedral and canonized as a saint with a shrine which became a resort for pilgrims seeking a cure for various kinds of diseases. Among those who were restored to health was Egwin the Saxon lord of Lydbury, and in gratitude he presented his manor to the Bishop of Hereford. It proved a useful stronghold, especially as it was flanked by Bishop's Moat two miles to the west and by another fortress, Lea Castle, on the east.[1]

The site of the now vanished bishop's castle is occupied by a hotel, and near it towards the top of the steep High Street is an eighteenth-century Town Hall with an interestingly prim façade. Beside it a narrow cobbled passage is straddled by the 'house on crutches' with its upper storey supported on two wooden posts. The church is at the lower end of the town and here there is a gravestone near the belfry door with an inscription unexpectedly written in French. It is obviously a memorial to a prisoner of war billeted here during the Napoleonic wars. It would be interesting to know who was responsible for setting up the stone and what poignant story undoubtedly lies behind these simple words recording the death of a middle-aged French soldier in a remote Shropshire village far from his native land –

A la mémoire de Louis Paces, Lieut. Colonel de chevaux légers, chevalier des ordres militaires des deux Siciles et de l'Espagne, mort à Bishop's Castle le 1er mai, 1814, âgé de 40 ans.

As in the case of many other Shropshire parishes the church records for several centuries are still preserved, and for the year 1593 there is an entry in Latin recording a virulent outbreak of the plague which the writer plainly attributed to the godlessness of the village. In translation it reads:

At this time God began to chastise us with his severe chastisement so that there died one hundred and seventy-four persons, men, women and children snatched away by a most heavy and violent disease and contagion of pestilence. God thought good thus to afflict us but we violated the holy Sabbath, for on the 24th of June, being the Lord's Day, the bailiffs and chief inhabitants

1 Bishop's Moat now shows only the gorse-covered outline of its earthworks. The scanty ruins of Lea Castle adjoin a farmhouse.

of this borough consented that markets should be held on that day, whereof they were taken like thieves in the very act.

In 1837 Bishop's Castle was reported as having 'twenty beer shops and no Sunday School' but it did have a whipping-post for local miscreants which seems to have been in fairly constant use. In the middle of the nineteenth century this particular parochial instrument of punishment was the occasion of an incident which provided a subject of mirth for many years. A hardened old reprobate who was well known in the neighbourhood as a notorious law breaker was tried at Shrewsbury assizes for theft, and was sentenced to be punished at Bishop's Castle's whipping-post. The old man's appearance belied his real character, for with his long flowing white hair and beard he had an imposing and patriarchal look. At the time it so happened that the popular Victorian artist Frederick Goodall was visiting Bishop's Castle. Goodall had made a name for himself as the painter of such pictures as *The Tired Soldier, Raising the Maypole, The Nubian Slave* and paintings of biblical subjects. Passing by the whipping-post when the old man was about to have his punishment he was much struck by the venerable appearance of the culprit. He made a quick sketch of his features and later painted an excellent portrait of him, not at the whipping-post but with his eyes looking heavenwards and his hands clasped in prayer. The picture, given the title of *Grace Before Meat*, was sold for a considerable sum and engravings of it were hung in hundreds of pious Victorian households, much to the amusement of people in and around Bishop's Castle who knew only too well that the original of the now famous portrait was anything but the devout paterfamilias he represented. The old man himself, however, was vastly proud of his sudden elevation to pictorial fame and is said to have earned many quarts of ale from strangers who heard him recount with suitable embellishments and omissions how he became a model for a famous artist.

The town of Clun is spread over the banks of the river which gives its name not only to the town but also to the castle, the forest and, as it flows eastwards, to a group of villages and hamlets –

> Clunton and Clunbury, Clungunford and Clun,
> Are the quietest places under the sun,

as one version of the old saying goes, although the adjective is often altered to 'dirtiest', 'drunkenest', and so on according to the fancy and mood of the speaker. At Clun the river runs under an ancient and picturesque saddle-backed bridge with five low arches separated by projecting angled piers which provide convenient recesses for pedestrians to take refuge from the traffic. The need to keep a look-out for hazards has prompted a local saying, 'whoever crosses Clun Bridge comes home sharper than he went'.

Of the castle and its fortifications there remain an impressive ruined Norman keep and some still formidable earthworks. The keep is a rectangular tower built on the edge of a great mound; about eighty feet high and with walls eleven feet thick it had three storeys and each floor had five windows and a fireplace. The entrance door was on the south side and a mural staircase led to the three floors. On the north and west sides the fortress was defended by the horseshoe bend of the river; on the south and east there was the ditch and defensive outworks of three platforms separated by moats. Clun Castle has always been regarded as the original of the Garde Doloureuse in *The Betrothed* which Scott describes as

A place strong by nature and well fortified by art, which the Welsh prince had found it impossible to conquer either by force or stratagem; and which, remaining with a strong garrison in his rear, often checked his invasions by rendering his retreat precarious. The river whose stream washes on three sides the base of the proud eminence on which the castle is situated, curves away from the fortress and its corresponding village on the west and the hill sinks downwards to an extensive plain, so extremely level as to indicate its alluvial origin. The bridge, a high narrow combination of arches of unequal size, was about half a mile distant from the castle, in the very centre of the plain. The river itself ran in a deep rocky channel, was often unfordable, and at all times difficult of passage, giving considerable advantage to the defenders of the castle.

There is drama enough in the true history of this grim-looking ruin, the stronghold of the Fitz-Alans, one of whom played such a valiant part against Stephen on behalf of Matilda, and in her cause lost all but his reputation as a resolute and loyal fighter. The real or supposed association of the castle with Scott's novel gives it an additional touch of romance as the place where

that trusty knight Sir Raymond Berenger fought his fatal battle with the wild tribes of Wales; where sorrowed the Lady Eveline, watched from afar by Damian de Lacy and attended by Rose the honest daughter of the doughty Fleming, Wilkin Flammock. Here Father Aldrovand, a monk of Wenlock Priory, rekindled his military fire; and here it was that the butler replied to the bibulous weaver that March and October 'for thirty years he had dealt with the best barley in Shropshire'.

Hare considers that Clun Castle does not fit Scott's description; for one thing the river is here too 'infantine'. The name Garde Doloureuse is borrowed from Malory so it is possible that the fortress itself existed only in his imagination although it has often been said, without any real evidence, that the novelist wrote part of *The Betrothed* at an inn at Clun. His only direct reference to a possible connection with Clun is somewhat ambiguous:

To requite this hospitality Raymond invited the Prince of Powys, with a chosen but limited train, during the ensuing Christmas, to the Garde Doloureuse which the antiquaries have endeavoured to identifiy with the Castle of Clun on the river of the same name. But the length of time and some geographical difficulties throw doubt on this ingenious conjecture.

This appears at first sight to demolish any claims the castle may have to be the original of Scott's castle but, as F. J. Snell rightly points out[1], if this is so,

why should Scott have inserted this apparently needless comment?

1   *The Celtic Borderland.*

It would seem after all that he was thinking of Clun Castle, but in a vague and wide sense enabling him to elude criticism to which he would otherwise have been liable. The adoption of a fictitious name from the Arthurian cycle gave him perfect freedom in any statements he chose to make.

A straggling street winds up the hill opposite the castle towards the church which itself has a massive squat tower worthy of a castle fortress, a reminder of the protection it may often have provided for the less able-bodied, non-combatant inhabitants of this continually threatened border town. It is a handsome building inside; occupied by Parliamentary forces during the Civil War it was partly burnt in a battle with the Royalists and after the Restoration Charles II ordered a national collection to be made to pay for repairs to the damage. To this date belongs the great west door which as a result was given the name of the Royal Door. The magnificence of the Jacobean pulpit always impresses me and there is a rare treasure here – the baldachino over the altar which is described as a 'pyx canopy'.

Something else well worth seeing inside the church is an unusual painting of its patron, Saint George, by an Abyssinian artist, a spirited and inspired memorial to a member of the Thesiger family who was killed on active service in 1942. Two older memorials are in the churchyard and are unusual in a different way. One dated 1811 records the deaths of

Edith Hamar	who died	August	20th	aged	14
Mary Hamar	,, ,,	,,	22nd	,,	18
Martha Hamar	,, ,,	,,	27th	,,	24
Aaron Hamar	,, ,,	,,	28th	,,	11
Edward Hamar	,, ,,	September	1st	,,	16
Jane Hamar	,, ,,	,,	4th	,,	4
George Hamar	,, ,,	,,	9th	,,	22

This tragic list concludes with the words,

The above children of Moses and Edith Hamar of Colesty in the parish were all carried off by a putrid fever in the short space of three weeks – a sad instance of the uncertainty of human life.

The other epitaph is to the memory of 'Charles Dilke, gentleman, of Mainstone who died 1825, aet. 45' –

> Joyous his birth, wealth o'er his cradle shone,
> Generous he proved, far was his bounty known,
> Men, horses, hounds were feasted at his hall;
> There strangers found a welcome, bed and stall;
> Quick distant idlers answered to his horn,
> And all was gladness in the sportsman's morn.
>
> But evening came and cold blew the gale,
> Means overdrawn had now begun to fail;
> His wine was finished and he ceased to brew,
> And fickle friends now hid them from his view,
> Unknown, neglected, pined the man of worth,
> Death his best friend, his resting place the earth.

The church has a brass memorial to Sir Robert Howard who is chiefly remembered for the romantic attachment he formed for the already married daughter of Edward Coke the famous seventeenth-century lawyer. The unhappy girl had been married against her will and returned Howard's love, but the course of this true love did not run smooth and his infatuation landed him in the court of the Star Chamber. Another member of the family has a different kind of memorial on the eastern edge of the town where Henry Howard, Earl of Northampton, in 1614 founded the Hospital of the Holy and Undivided Trinity as a 'refuge for decayed tradesmen'. It is a charming group of stone cottages arranged around a quadrangle enclosing a garden, and there is a chapel built in accordance with the founder's ordinance, 'We do ordain and establish that in the said Hospital there shall be, for ever, One Warden and Twelve Poor Men, who shall wholly give themselves to the Service of God, and to pray for the Peace, Tranquillity and Concord of all Christendom'.

The almshouses can now accommodate fifteen residents and in 1959 the Charity Commissioners drew up a new scheme for the administration of the Hospital more in line with the needs of modern conditions. Under the new arrangements, to fill vacancies the trustees choose 'poor men of good character' from the districts of Clun and Bishop's Castle, and from the Welsh parishes of Knighton and Church Stoke. In addition, for the first time, wives may reside and are allowed to remain in residence after their widowhood. Many of the residents nowadays pay a small rent for their quarters, and one attractive link with the past has now disappeared: they no longer wear their picturesque old uniform – a long grey gown on weekdays and on Sundays an ample blue version with the badge of their founder, a white lion, on the sleeve.

From Clun to Newcastle the road follows the river valley winding between rounded hills, some bare, some wooded, some cultivated with crops, and some with bracken covering their flanks up to the summits. The village of Newcastle lies below the beetling height of a prehistoric camp; we turn to the right below it, by the Crown Inn, and then strike northwards by taking the first lane to the left after passing the church. The road climbs steeply by the side of Offa's Dyke which runs along the flank of Craig Hill. As you are now high above the valley you can overlook typical Clun Forest scenery stretching away to the Welsh borderland.

We now go downwards between the hills and then climb up to Three Gates, where we take the road signposted to Colebatch. We then pass Shadwell Hall, a remote lonely house, and then turn left at the next crossroads. From now on it is a steady descent but before arriving at the village of Mainstone which lies deep in the valley of the little River Unk, turn left and continue to Churchtown. Here, hidden in another valley at the foot of Clun Forest, is Mainstone's church, a good mile away from the village. It is a simple aisleless building, and resting on the floor beside the pulpit is the smooth granite boulder from which the village is supposed to acquire its name. In former times it was the custom for the village youths to show their strength by heaving the stone above their heads and then casting it backwards over the left shoulder – quite a feat, as it is said to weigh something like two hundredweight.

Another interesting possession of the church is an old clarinet and bassoon which were bought in 1828 and for fifty years were used every Sunday to lead the singing. When I look at the double music stand which the players used and which has also been preserved, I can conjure up a vivid picture of the two rustic performers facing one another on opposite sides of this roughly made contraption which supported their dog-eared pieces of manuscript music. One of them would give the signal and they would start up the music, an ungainly but earnest duo, giving a false note now and again, but encouraging and supporting the wavering voices of the congregation. Just as they themselves were destined to be superseded by one of those 'barrel-organs or the things next door to 'em that you blow wi' your foot', so these two instruments may have replaced amateur string players, probably after a certain amount of healthy parochial opposition reminiscent of Hardy's *Under the Greenwood Tree* in which the tranter disagreed with the argument that the village church should have 'stuck to strings and kept out clarinets'. On the contrary he stoutly maintained that 'as far as look is concerned I don't for my part see that a fiddle is much nearer heaven than a clar'net. 'Tis further off. There's always a rakish, scampish twist about a fiddle's looks that seems to say the Wicked One had a hand in the making o' en; while angels be supposed to play clar'nets in heaven, or som'at like 'em, if ye may believe picters'.

This is Offa's Dyke territory; the great vallum and fosse of this ancient earthwork curve over Edenhope Hill and continue striding over the slope on the other side of the road which now mounts steeply, bordered by the sheer side of Cwm Ffrydd, a narrow valley as dramatic in its own way as Coleridge's 'deep romantic chasm which slanted down the green hill'. At the summit of the hill we are in a wide expanse of moorland scenery, wild perhaps, but invigorating and giving a heady sense of exhilaration. We continue straight over the crossroads at Two Crosses overlooking Wales and fold upon fold of mountains stretching away into the distance. At Brook House we keep right and start to climb again. At the next 'T' junction we turn right and pass over a cattle-grid for Crossways across an open lonely moorland.

At Crossways, after passing over another cattle-grid, our road turns left, but off a lane to the right beside a farm there is a rough track leading past the plantations of conifers to the Cantlin Cross and Stone. The finely carved Cross was set up by Beriah Botfield, a member of parliament for Ludlow, and has no particular history. The Stone is a flat slab of grey limestone roughly inscribed with the words,

W.C. DECSED HERE BURIED 1691 AT BETVS

and an odd story is told about it. The initials represent the name William Cantlin, a travelling pedlar who collapsed and died at this spot – another story says that he was murdered here. There was something of an argument among the neighbouring parishes as to the responsibility for burying the stranger, but finally Bettws-y-Crwyn agreed to give him a grave in their churchyard. Nearly two centuries later it was rewarded for its act of charity; on the passing of the Clun Forest Enclosure Act there had to be some readjustment of parish boundaries, and the irrefutable proof of the Cantlin Stone gave Bettws several hundred acres more than had been originally allotted to the parish.

Back on our road again we go straight over the crossroads passing by Badger Moor along the edge of Black Mountain with superb views of the Welsh mountains. Turn left at the next crossroads, and then left again until you reach a tiny chapel where you take the turning to the right. Then the church of Bettws-y-Crwyn is close by on the left. This simple building was put up centuries ago as a place of worship for the shepherds of the surrounding hills, or perhaps as a shrine beside the holy well which is below the church. Standing over 1,400 feet above sea level it must have one of the highest sites of any church in the whole of England. Certainly its tower stands 'four-square to all the winds that blow', which they do with piercing persistence here. Although so remote the church is obviously looked after with care and pride, and the simple sixteenth-century screen and the Jacobean pulpit are particularly appealing in this setting. On the ends of the solid oak benches are displayed the names of various farmhouses known locally as Halls – Hall of the Forest, Moor Hall, Cow Hall, and so on.

Continuing along the road we turn left to Stoney Pound past the telephone booth. This is another remarkable road; on one side a large area of Shropshire is spread out below like a gigantic relief map, and on the other there is the spectacular mountain scenery of Wales. Although we are making for Llanfair Waterdine, ignore the first signpost bearing its name and continue along a high shelf road. Ignore, too, the second signpost to Llanfair and go on to Springhill where you turn right and have a magnificent stretch of Offa's Dyke running along beside your road – a sombre and inscrutable relic of those savage days of inter-racial strife when the law enacted that any Welshman found east of the boundary should, the first time, lose his right hand, and for a subsequent offence, his head.

We begin to descend and as proof that we have left the wind-swept uplands we go through a leafy lane, over a gently rippling stream, through the melliflously named Cwm Collo and into a wooded valley beside a hill suitably called Mount Pleasant. Church and pub in Llanfair Waterdine seem to have come to terms by squarely facing each other on opposite sides of the road. I can say nothing about the inn as my visits to the village have never coincided with 'opening times'; of the church the chief thing to be said is that it was rather grimly restored in the second half of last century. Hanging on the wall is an old engraving, rather like a Dickens illustration by Phiz, which shows the delightful old building the restorers were set to work on. Fortunately they preserved a part of what must have been a wealth of good woodwork: a portion of the original screen, finely carved with foliage, bunches of grapes, figures of men and women and a lively collection of animals – pigs, rabbits, dogs and even a lion and a dragon. It now does duty as an altar rail and bears a cryptic inscription which has caused a good deal of learned controversy:

SYR MADE AMURAC PICHGAR COL UNW AGOSOD ODDEC
PUND CYRUFUDD

The generally accepted English version is 'Sir Matthew and Meyrick Pichgar of Clun set it[1] up for ten pounds together'.

The road continues along the bank of the River Teme and the boundary between Shropshire and Wales. Do not miss the turning to Stow, an unspoilt village in the magnificent setting of a miniature Swiss valley, clinging to the side of its hill below Holloway Rocks and high above the secluded valley. The east window of the church sheds a peaceful radiance with clear bright colours like those of some pre-Raphaelite water-colour, a refreshing change from the garish hues which all too often stare out of some nineteenth-century stained glass. Equally to my taste is the cleanly designed reredos and the two memorials in golden mosaic and alabaster. Nikolaus Pevsner remarks that they are suggestive of the Art Nouveau style; for me they suggest a rare, unaffected beauty of a more spacious age.

We end our tour of the Clun Forest district at Hopton Castle where the remains of a Norman keep stand on slightly rising ground in a fertile valley backed by swelling hills, making a scene so gentle and pastoral that it is difficult to believe this forlorn ruin was the scene of one of the most barbarous incidents in the whole history of the Civil War in Shropshire. On 22nd August 1642 Charles I had set up his standard, a large blood-red streamer with the royal arms and inscribed with the minatory words, 'Give to Caesar His Due', at Nottingham. Scarcely had it been fixed in its place when

a fierce gust of wind sweeping with a wild moan across the hill

1 That is, the rood screen of which it was originally a part.

laid it low and it was with difficulty raised again. This was looked on by many as prophetic of evil, and the standard was borne back to the castle in the evening in silence, and the stormy sky seemed to sympathize with the dark shadow that lay on all men's minds.

News of this inauspicious omen reached Shropshire in due course but meanwhile the king regarded the county as one of the strongholds of his cause, and all the principal castles and mansions were put in a state of defence, mostly on behalf of the Royalists. Before long, however, the demands on the innocent populace for free quartering of soldiers, victuals and other supplies, and the excesses committed by Royalists and Parliamentarians alike made ordinary folk cry 'a plague o' both your houses!' As one contemporary ruefully expressed it,

> I had six oxen t'other day,
> And them the Roundheads got away,
> A mischief to their speed.
> I had six horses in a hale,
> And them the Cavaliers stale;
> I think in this they be agreed.

Considering the misery that was thus inflicted on the county it is not surprising that those who were so harassed and oppressed became indifferent as to which of their tormentors prevailed. In fact at one period it was reported that the men of Clun and Bishop's Castle 'about a thousand of them in arms are standing out against both sides, neither for the king nor for the parliament, but stand only upon their own guard for the preservation of their lives and fortunes'.

Unfortunately Hopton Castle was unable to stand aside from the war. It was the property of one of the most rabid Roundheads in the whole county and at the very outset of the conflict had been garrisoned for Parliament with a handful of men under the command of Colonel Samuel More with a Major Phillips as his deputy. In a diary which survived the vicissitudes of his career Colonel More recorded the calamitous course of the garrison's gallant struggle against hopeless odds.

I went to Hopton Castle on the 18th of February, 1643 which was the Sabbath Day, at night. The next night the Royalists came before it who facing us with a body of horse first, within an hour sent a body of foot who approached the outer walls. They brought ladders to scale the walls but upon our killing three of them they sent Major Sutton to tell me the Prince demanded the delivery of the castle. I sent word that I understood no message that comes without drum or trumpet. Thereupon they sent a summons by a drum subscribed by Sir Michael Woodhouse who demanded the castle in the name of Prince Rupert. My answer was that I kept it by authority of Parliament and by consent of the owner for King and Parliament.

For a whole fortnight the small beleagured fortress held out against a number of sharp sallies and sudden attacks. Then the Royalists brought up two heavy guns and a summons was sent to the castle that if Colonel More did not surrender before the first shot from a gun he and his men must expect no quarter, in accordance with the accepted rule of war that those who wilfully attempt to hold an indefensible position are punished by death.

Colonel More returned a defiant answer which infuriated the besiegers who had already lost a number of men and had many more wounded. They opened fire and the first shots killed one of the garrison and wounded two more as well as making some impression on the walls which the attacking force then proceeded to mine. It soon became obvious to Colonel More that his exhausted men could hold out no longer.

Our men, weary of working all night and not out of their clothes for a fortnight's time, it was moved we should desire a parley which being done they bade us send our conditions which Major Phillips and I contrived to this effect, that we should march away with our arms and ammunition, which they denied. We agreed then to propose to the enemy we should yield the castle upon quarter for our lives. Answer was brought that no other condition could be yielded to, but to be referred to Colonel Woodhouse's mercy. Being brought to this condition it was thought better to yield than be blown up. But indeed we all thought we should only be made prisoners and did not think of such a death as hereafter appears.

Colonel More was taken to Ludlow Castle as a prisoner; Major Phillips offered twenty pounds to save his own life but this was refused, and the horrible sequel to the surrender was related in a contemporary news-sheet:

The barbarous and unparalleled murder committed at Hopton Castle deserves to be recorded in letters of blood to all posterities. The truth is that Master More having under his command twenty-four soldiers defended that place severall days and nights against the continual alarmes and assaults of the enemy and at length despairing of relief, and having no possibility of holding it out, he had parley with the enemy and surrendered the castle. Major More was seized upon and carried away prisoner and the twenty-four soldiers tied back to back, and then some of them had their hands cut off; some with a hand, parte of an arme, and the rest cut and mangled both on hands and armes, and then all of them throne into a muddy pit where as often as any of them endeavoured to raise themselves out of the mud, striving to prolong their miserable lives, they were straight by these bloody villains beate down into the mud again with great stones and in this sad manner lamentably perished.

This was a Parliamentarian report, biased no doubt, but as proof that this grisly deed was in fact perpetrated a dejected entry in the parish register records the fate of these wretched men,

Occisi fuere 29 in castro Hoptoniensi inter quos Henricus Gregorye, senex, et comeranneus meus.

Thus ended Hopton Castle's unhappy role in the great Civil War about which, when peace at last came, one disenchanted observer wrote, 'After the expense of so much blood and treasure all the difference between our former and our present state is that before, under the complaints of a slavery we lived like Freemen, and now under the notions of a freedom we live like Slaves'.

Chapter 8

The Shropshire lass and lad

It was G. K. Chesterton who suggested that if A. E. Housman is to be identified with the *Shropshire Lad* then the work of the novelist Mary Webb 'might be called the prose poems of a Shropshire Lass'. Her books are in fact good examples of what the French classify as *romans régionalistes*; 'she has the love of earth epitomized in one special corner of earth; a profound faith in men and women epitomized in the diverse group who peopled the Shropshire she wrote about'.[1] For her this love of the county where she was born was an abiding passion; it coloured all her emotions and her writing; it was the inspiration and the setting of her novels; and it was the ever-present influence which suffused the best of her poetry.

Gladys Meredith – her second name Mary was used only after her marriage – was born in 1881 at Leighton, a small village below the southern slopes of the Wrekin. She was the first child of George Edward Meredith who rather late in life had married the daughter of an Edinburgh doctor. The father was obviously an important formative influence in the life of his daughter, and he is said to be the original of John Arden in *The Golden Arrow* 'whose brown thin face ran into kindly smiles as easily as a brook runs in its accustomed bed'. He was the son and grandson of former

1 Thomas Moult *Mary Webb, Her Life and Work.*

vicars of Leighton but he himself chose to live the life of a minor country gentleman which he contrived to do with some small independent means eked out by tutoring candidates for the universities and Sandhurst. There seems to have been a touch of harmless easy-going fecklessness in his nature, and one of the features of the Meredith family life was the number of times they moved house. From Leighton they went to The Grange in Much Wenlock, then later to Woodlands (now Harcourt Manor) at Stanton-on-Hine Heath, and from there to Meole Brace where their house Maesbrook still stands but is much changed by rebuilding.

Mrs Meredith's influence on her eldest daughter was not so much formative as destructive. Thomas Moult's tactful biography of Mary Webb describes her mother as a noble-minded, warm-hearted person whose 'idea of duty, justice and honour was paramount in her lengthy life'. A very different picture emerges from Dorothy P. H. Wrenn's excellent life of the novelist in which Mrs Meredith stands out clearly as an unamiable, cold and selfish woman, indifferent towards her children, 'resentful of her belated maternity', and finally taking refuge in hypochondria and some kind of mysterious imaginary illness which conveniently confined her to her bedroom, and removed her from family and social life for five years, when it suddenly suited her to take charge of the household once again.

During the years that her mother was the *malade imaginaire* most of the household's responsibilities fell upon Gladys Meredith and a much-loved governess. The first child of the family, separated by some six years from the eldest of the other five children, she grew up serious beyond her years, yet with a zest for the simple enjoyments of country life, and an especially vivid appreciation of the beauties of nature. 'As a child', she wrote in *The Spring of Joy*, 'I remember standing awe-stricken at the strange beauty of a well-known field in the magic of a June dawn.' At a quite early age she showed a flair for writing and was producing verses and short plays for performance by local children. Then at the age of twenty she was struck down by ill-health, which dogged her at intervals for the rest of her life. Her fever, weakness and palpitations were finally diagnosed as the symptoms of exophthalmic goitre, the disease which, together with pernicious anaemia, caused her death at an early age. Her enforced idleness and the long days she had to spend lying on a couch beside a window with a view of the Shropshire hills proved a decisive period for the career as a writer she had secretly determined to follow. More ambitious verses and essays were attempted, and the latter were later used as the basis of the studies of nature published in 1917 under the title *The Spring of Joy*.

She made a slow recovery from this illness but in 1909 there was a temporary but serious relapse due partly to her grief at the sudden death of her father whose companionship and sympathetic affection had been, perhaps unwisely too exclusively, the centre of her emotional life. Meanwhile she had made some new friends at Meole Brace, among them a schoolmaster H. B. L. Webb in whom she found an understanding companion with ideas and tastes similar to her own. After a short time their engagement was announced, and in 1912 when she was thirty-one years of age they were married in the parish church at Meole Brace.[1]

A photograph of Mary Webb in her early teens shows a face of 'strength and determination, acute sensitiveness, independence, candour and humour'; after her illness, her protruding eyes, the swelling of the goitre in her neck and her sickly complexion gave her a less pleasing appearance of which she grew increasingly and sensitively conscious. The couple spent the first two years of their married life at Weston-super-Mare in Somerset where he had obtained a post in a preparatory school. For Mary Webb these were years of exile which made her realize that she could be happy only in her native county. Finally, with supreme indifference to the practical difficulties entailed they decided (or she decided for

1 A brass plate on a pew records that 'Mary Webb worshipped here 1902–1912'.

him) that he should give up teaching and return to Shropshire to live on their scanty savings and her mother's allowance, eked out with money made by selling garden produce. Another addition to their income would be from writing, not only the books Mary planned but also literary work by her husband, who was himself an author in his own right and under the pseudonym of J. Clayton wrote a trilogy of novels about thirteenth-century France, *Gold of Toulouse*, *Dew in April* and *Anger of the North*. The decision once taken, the Webbs hurriedly left Weston at the end of the summer term in 1914 and moved into Rose Cottage, a small house at Pontesbury with a large garden; it can still be seen, although somewhat altered and renamed Roseville, just outside the village near the railway bridge. The inexpert Henry laboured in the garden with commendable persistence and Mary, carelessly dressed 'in an old coat and a faded gown', doggedly sold, or failed to sell, the fruit, flowers and vegetables every week at a stall in Shrewsbury market.

It seems an odd way of making a living for such a couple to choose. They had both been brought up in middle-class comfort and in educated households, and they were both inexperienced in practical affairs. It is hardly surprising that having to live the penurious life of labouring folk they were now generally ignored by their social equals, and regarded as weird eccentrics by the rest of the villagers who decided that they had come down in the world through their own blameworthy shiftlessness. This social isolation did not worry Mary Webb, and her experience of life as a stall-holder at Shrewsbury market was not wasted. Indeed, it heightened her already perceptive appreciation of the various facets making up the characters of the Shropshire country folk she came into contact with.

Meanwhile her return to Shropshire had already proved an inspiration for her writing; and the strange crouching shape of the nearby Pontesford Hill and its ancient legend[1] fired her imagination.

1   *See page* 102.

As a result she completed in three weeks the draft of her first novel, *The Golden Arrow*, which was published in 1916. All the weakness and strength of her writing are well exemplified in this book, and its theme, like those of her later novels, is developed more by atmosphere and poetical imagination than by action. It tells a simple story of two pairs of lovers and their parents. The ardent, generous-hearted Deborah Arden is linked with the unbalanced, impetuous Stephen Southernwood who 'hated to be tied' and discovered after marriage that 'a blight' fell on his love for her. The trivial, selfish Lily Huntbatch who marries Deborah's clumsy but devoted brother Joe provides the foil to Deborah. The contrasting courses of these couples' loves run in effective juxtaposition and although, as might be expected in a first novel, the characterization is weak, yet the four main young characters and the father, John Arden, are drawn with a vividness and vigour which constitute a remarkable achievement for a prentice hand. Other characters, like the shrill Mrs Arden and the misanthropic Eli Huntbatch, are less successful and only rarely show up as anything more than stock caricatures; but the essential strength of the book, as of her other novels, lies not in the plot but in the glowing sincerity of the descriptive writing. The writer reveals herself as a precise and poetical observer and interpreter of nature with 'senses almost microscopic in their delicacy', as Walter de la Mare expressed it. Matched with this poetic sensibility is an equally effective uncompromising realism inspiring descriptions like that of the butcher's stall in the market at Shrewsbury, thinly disguised in the book as 'Silverton':

Beauty was everywhere, except in the meat market. There slow bluebottles, swollen and unwholesome, crawled and buzzed; men of a like complexion shouted stertorously, brandishing stained carving-knives; an unbearable stench arose from the offal, and women with pretty clothes and refined manners bought the guts of animals under such names as 'sweetbreads' or 'prime fat kidneys', and thrust their hands into the disembowelled bodies of rabbits to test their freshness.

131

The influence of personal experience on Mary Webb's work is well illustrated in this first novel with its setting of local Shropshire places. Here the Stiperstones figure as the 'Diafol Mountain'; Ratlinghope is 'Slepe'; Church Stretton is given the name 'Shepwardine'; the Long Mynd appears as 'Wilderhope'; and Bishop's Castle is easily identifiable under its fictional name of 'Mallard's Keep'. And at the very heart of the book there lurks the sinister brooding influence of the Devil's Chair on the Stiperstones which stands

bleak, massive, untenanted, yet with a well-worn air. It had the look of a chair from which the occupant has just risen, to which he will shortly return. It was understood that only when vacant could the throne be seen. Whenever rain, sleet or mist made a grey shechinah there people said, 'There's harm brewing.' 'He's in his chair.' Not that they talked of it much; they simply felt it, as sheep feel the coming of the snow.

The Golden Arrow attracted surprisingly little attention from the critics and brought in very little money to its author. The Webbs moved from Rose Cottage into a still cheaper and more primitive cottage, The Nills, hidden under the northern slopes of the Stiperstones. Much to Henry Webb's relief his wife at last agreed that it was impossible to earn a living by amateur market gardening and he obtained a teaching post in Chester. Here they lived with her mother who had recently moved from Shropshire in order to be near one of Mary's married sisters. It was not a happy time for the long-suffering Henry Webb. During the week he would return from work to find himself having to act as a peace-making buffer between the antagonistic temperaments of his wife and mother-in-law; and every weekend Mary insisted on their returning to The Nills where he had to perform most of the household chores while she was busily engaged on her next novel, which was published in 1917.

John Buchan has described *Gone to Earth* as 'partly allegory' with a story of 'the clash of common lusts and petty jealousies'.

Once again the plot is extremely thin: Hazel Woodus is the wild, self-willed motherless daughter of a gipsy woman and a cranky beekeeper, harpist and coffin-maker. Improbably enough she marries Edward Marston, a solemn, idealistic and somewhat inadequate minister but, 'driven by a strange inner power' and with surprisingly ready acquiescence, she gives herself to the lust of Jack Reddin, the dissolute squire of Undern Hall who has already fathered a brood of illegitimate children by a sluttish, insolent mistress, Sally Haggard. Hazel was 'fascinated by Reddin; she was drawn to confide in Edward; but she wanted neither of them. Whether or not in years to come she would find room in her heart for human passion, she had no room for it now. She had only room for the little creatures she befriended, and for her eager, quickly growing self.' The book is mostly old-fashioned melodrama, at times pitched in an impossibly high key, but the character of Hazel Woodus with her burning hatred of all forms of cruelty and her infinite love and pity for persecuted and hunted wild creatures, is convincingly drawn, and the general gloom of the book is relieved by two outstanding scenes – the heroine's journey to her wedding in a farm-cart, and the picture of the wedding itself.

Some of the minor characters, too, like Reddin's manservant Andrew Vessous, Mrs Marston and the Miss Clombers sometimes jerk out of their puppet-like motions and move with an independent life of their own; and as in her previous novel the Shropshire countryside is portrayed with artistic precision and sympathy. We are given subtle descriptions of lambent beauty like that of Hazel in the churchyard at dawn:

It was as if the dead had arisen in the stark hours between twelve and two, and were waiting unobtrusively, majestically, each by his own bed, to go down and break their long fast with the bee and the grass-snake in refectories too minute and too immortal to be known by the living. The tombstones seemed taller, seemed to have a presence behind them; the lush grass, lying grey and heavy with dew, seemed to have been swept by silent passing crowds.

Strangely enough, in the context of melodrama, the description of Hazel's tragic end as she fell to her death over the quarry's edge, still shielding her pet fox from the pursuing pack of hounds, is a masterpiece of word economy, and genuinely moving, even though it is the most melodramatic incident in the book. It achieves its effect without cheap emotion, and the simple epitaph 'She was gone with Foxy into everlasting silence' sounds the most impressively pathetic note of the whole story.

By 1918 the strain of the family disagreements at Chester and of travelling to and from The Nills at weekends made Henry Webb decide to accept a teaching post at The Priory School in Shrewsbury. Ever since the time when the Merediths lived at Meole Brace Mary Webb had regarded Lyth Hill, some three miles south of Shrewsbury, as the ideal place for a house. With the aid of an advance from her mother and a mortgage loan from the bank a small plot of land was purchased on the summit of the hill. She herself drew up the plans of a small bungalow which she called Spring Cottage; a modest enough place with only three rooms but with magnificent views of the Shropshire countryside she loved and wrote about. The bungalow is still standing, but altered and enlarged since Mary Webb's time.

The move into Spring Cottage made this one of the happiest periods of Mary Webb's life, and her content is reflected in parts of her novel *The House in Dormer Forest* which in spite of certain literary and artistic flaws I find one of her most satisfying books, with some unforced humorous touches to offset the sombre gloom of what is really the central character – the house itself, 'a mansion to the majority, a prison to the few'. The plot, in so far as it can be called a plot, revolves around an ill-assorted family living together in uneasy proximity, stifled by an atmosphere of pharisaical conformity and subservience to convention. Much of the material is a repetition of ideas used in the author's previous novels. Dormer House, obviously situated in the countryside around Minsterley, is strongly reminiscent of Undern Hall; and

Ruby Darke presents another facet of Lily Huntbatch, just as her sister Amber is a more fully developed character study of Deborah Arden, as well as being something of a reflection of Mary Webb herself, whose 'manner, when she was at ease, had charm, but it was spoilt by shyness. Her hair was of an indeterminate brown, and her complexion was ruined by ill-health, due to the perpetual chafing of the wistful mind longing for things not in Dormer'. The parents, Solomon and Rachel Darke, and the two sons Peter and Jasper, are all effectively contrasted, and the grandmother Mrs Velindre is one of the writer's most successful creations. In addition, the book has a strikingly lifelike character in the malevolent Catherine Velindre, a distant relative who lives with the family, while the portrait of the odious clergyman, Ernest Swyndle, is sketched with a bitter animosity that seems almost to strike a personal note. The narrative limps in places, and there is a certain amount of false pathos and improbable lovemaking; it is impossible, for example, really to believe in the romantic meeting and whirlwind courtship of Amber Darke and Michael Hallowes; and Jasper Darke's incongruous reappearance after his supposed suicide is equally a strain on the reader's credulity. Even with these blemishes, however, the book is obviously the work of a talented writer with an individual style sufficiently strongly marked to inspire Stella Gibbons's *Cold Comfort Farm,* a brilliantly sustained parody which shrewdly mimics the form and characters of the novel.

Shortly after the publication of *The House in Dormer Forest* in 1920 Mary Webb fell ill again. For hours she sat listless and despondent, unable to write, and neglectful of her personal appearance and housekeeping duties. Morbidly suspicious of strangers, especially those of her own sex, she was fiercely, almost pathologically, jealous of her husband who found it impossible to have any normal social contacts owing to her unreasonable possessiveness. In an attempt to cure her of what appeared to be acute depression and a certain amount of hypochondria inherited from her mother, Henry Webb moved to a teaching appointment at Golders Green in London where he hoped his wife would be diverted by meeting other writers and so enlarge her own literary horizon. Spring Cottage was kept for the holidays; when in London they lived in a tiny furnished house in Hampstead.

By now Mary Webb had a small but discerning reading public and she met a number of celebrities, among them Lady Asquith, Mrs Thomas Hardy, Evelyn Underhill, Walter de la Mare and Stephen Graham. For a time the variety and excitement of this new life in London improved her health but soon she was pining to return to Shropshire, and poems like *To a Blackbird Singing in London* convey the aching nostalgia which filled every week she was away from Lyth Hill:

> Sing on, dear bird! Bring the old rapturous pain,
> In this great town where I no welcome find.
> Show me the murmuring forest in your mind,
> And April's fragile cups, brimful of rain.
> O sing me far away, that I may hear
> The voice of grass and, weeping, may be blind
> To slights and lies and friends that prove unkind.

She began to spend more and more time at Spring Cottage while her husband during term time had to remain in London, returning for occasional weekends to Lyth Hill only to find the house neglected and Mary Webb in a mood of unjust recrimination and jealous suspicion which often provoked an open quarrel. Something of this tortured unhappiness of her mind entered into her fourth novel *Seven for a Secret* which was dedicated by permission to 'the illustrious name of Thomas Hardy'. The story is set in Clun country disguised under the somewhat clumsy name of Dysgwlfas-on-the-Wild-Moors, 'the country that lies between the dimpled lands of England and the gaunt purple steeps of Wales – half in Faery and half out of it'. Action again is reduced to a minimum and the mixture of dramatic situation is much the same as in Mary Webb's other novels, with a contrast between Gillian

Lovekin's romantic love for the honest cowman-shepherd Robert Rideout, and her sensual infatuation with the sordid innkeeper Ralph Elmer who seduces her with little opposition on her part because 'a vitality greater than their own rushed through their veins and pounded in their breasts'. We have met these three characters before under different names, as well as a number of the subsidiary characters; but a new subtle characterization is presented in Rwth, the tragic dumb servant-woman who is secretly married to Elmer; and in the helpless, lovable Jonathan Makepeace whose comic tragedy was 'that since he had first held a rattle, inanimate matter had been his foe'. The essayist Robert Lynd remarks that 'a tempestuous energy storms through the landscape of *Seven for a Secret*'; it might be added that for all this energy and its accompanying poetic intensity, 'sympathy, pity and awe', the novel clearly shows that the author had not yet acquired the invaluable art of rendering the improbable not only probable but natural.

When Mary Webb was writing her next book her health had seriously deteriorated; her exophthalmic goitre and pernicious anaemia were steadily sapping her strength and her husband was warned that there was no hope of her recovery. Yet *Precious Bane*, her last completed novel, was also her best, showing her at the height of her powers. Although she had not been told of her condition she seemed to sense that her time was short, and in this book she evokes with passionate, urgent intensity the atmosphere of beauty and mystery surrounding the Shropshire countryside, its folklore, dialect and local customs which had been woven into the very tissue of her reveries since childhood. It is a story of memorable characters and exceptional situations but there is no sense of strain in the writing; the theme is well controlled and the author shows an unexpected mastery of the special technical difficulties of a narrative written in the first person.

The central character is the ruthless Gideon Sarn who is obsessed by his desire of material gain, and nothing is allowed to stand in the way of his attaining his object. He might have chosen 'the path of love and merry days', but instead he took 'the path of strange twists and turns where was the thing of dread, the bane, the precious bane, that feeds on life-blood'. He exploits his sister, murders his mother when she is no longer able to work, and rejects his love-child and Jancis Beguildy who 'was his wife, all but the ring'. Retribution follows when he faces ruin after a disastrous fire, and when he is haunted by the memory of those he has wronged. As the mists close in over his reason he rows over Sarn Mere[1] to the place where the figure of Jancis Beguildy seems to beckon him and where 'none was ever found that went in'; and the watchers on the shore saw the empty boat drift back, 'stealing in, slow, slow'.

This 'story of us all at Sarn, of Mother and Gideon and me, and Jancis (that was so beautiful), and Wizard Beguildy, and the two or three other folk that lived in those parts' is told by Prue Sarn, a gentle selfless girl who suffers for her plainness and her disfiguring harelip. From the very first chapter written when Prue was 'a very old woman and a tired woman, with a task to do before she says good-night to this world', we realize that this is Mary Webb herself speaking, and Prue's role in the story is suffused with a kind of spiritual radiancy culminating in the lyrical ecstasy of her final discovery of love and 'the peace to which all hearts do strive' with Kester Woodseaves. He, too, is a portrait from life, for he can be none other than Henry Webb, who – in spite of all misunderstandings – was, in the words of her two dedications to him, 'a noble lover', and 'whose presence is home'.

With a few exceptions the critics were lukewarm in their reviews of *Precious Bane*, but she did receive two recognitions which gave her much happiness in her last months. The novel was awarded the Femina Vie Heureuse Prize for 1924–5, a prize given annually for 'the best work of imagination in prose or verse descriptive of English life by an author who has not gained sufficient recognition'.

1 Mary Webb's fictional name for the lake of Bomere near Lyth Hill.

The other acknowledgment was from the Prime Minister, Stanley Baldwin, who had been given a copy of the book as a Christmas present in 1926. He wrote from Downing Street to express his delight with it; his ancestors had lived for centuries in Shropshire and 'I read it at Christmas within sight of the Clee Hills, at home. Thank you a thousand times for it'. Mary Webb's grateful reply mentioned that she was then engaged on a novel 'about the Welsh Marches just after the Norman Conquest', but this book, *Armour Wherein He Trusted*, written in a not wholly successful pseudo-medieval tushery, was never completed. Stanley Baldwin had given pleasure to a dying woman only just in time; nine months later at the age of forty-six she died in a nursing home at St Leonards-on-Sea.

In the following year during a speech at the Royal Literary Fund dinner Stanley Baldwin expressed his surprise that a novelist of Mary Webb's genius should be so neglected. As a result of this she became almost overnight a fashionable vogue, and for a time her novels enjoyed an exaggerated popularity both here and in America. At present it is rather more difficult to decide the exact place she should occupy among English novelists. She was perhaps at heart a regionalist poet who had chosen to write novels in prose – unrivalled within their limits – about a region she knew intimately, the Shropshire Marchland where Celts and Saxons had intermingled. As she herself wrote,

Shropshire is a county where the dignity and beauty of ancient things lingers long, and I have been fortunate not only in being born and brought up in its magical atmosphere, and in having many friends in farm and cottage who, by pleasant talk and reminiscence have fired the imagination, but also in having a mind as was my father's – a mind stored with old tales and legends that did not come from books, and rich with an abiding love for the beauty of forest and harvest field, all the more intense, perhaps, because it found little opportunity of expression.

And in fact these 'peoples and traditions and turns of speech and proverbial wisdom is what Mary Webb saw with the eye of the mind as she stood at her stall in Shrewsbury market, fastened in her memory, and fashioned for us in the little parcel of novels which is her legacy to literature'.[1]

Whereas Mary Webb was born and brought up in Shropshire A. E. Housman was a native of Worcestershire. He was born in 1859 at Fockbury, a small hamlet near Bromsgrove, and it was only an idealized sentiment for the neighbouring county which fortuitously suggested the local setting of *A Shropshire Lad*. He was the eldest child of a family of seven and seems never to have had much affection for his father, a colourless, ineffectual man whose indolence and later intemperance cost him his solicitor's practice, and ultimately caused the shabby gentility of their family life to be still further reduced to financial stringency. His wife had to shoulder the responsibility of managing the precarious household economy, bringing up the children and generally keeping up appearances. Housman was greatly devoted to her, and her death when he was only twelve years old was a bitter blow to a boy already aloof and abnormally sensitive. Shortly before this he had won a scholarship to Bromsgrove School where he proved an outstanding scholar, regularly carrying off prizes in English verse, classics and French. Reserved and shy, he showed his occasional cheerful moods only to a very few, mostly his family. He appears to have made no intimate friends at school and when he was not reading he spent his spare time taking solitary walks and exploring the Worcestershire countryside. The vigorous independence of his mind may be gauged from his confesson in later life that he was a deist at the age of thirteen, and a convinced atheist when he was twenty-one.

In 1877 Housman was awarded a scholarship at Saint John's College Oxford to read classics, and his future career not only seemed secure but also provided the one certain hope of the family.

1   Stanley Baldwin.

At Bromsgrove he had become a hero-worshipper of the head-master, a handsome, forceful figure, so very different from Housman's effete and spineless father. It was a hero-worship natural enough in an impressionable schoolboy, but perhaps rather more significant when taken in conjunction with his untypically candid confession, about the same time, of his admiration for the equally virile and impressive guardsmen whom he had seen on a visit to London, and who may well have inspired the lines he wrote later in *A Shropshire Lad*:

> The street sounds to the soldiers' tread,
>   And out we troop to see;
> A single redcoat turns his head,
>   He turns and looks at me.

Perhaps Housman himself half resented the admiration the soldiers aroused in him – 'barbarian' is his description of it – but they represented substitute-figures for all that he could never be, and all that his father never was, and released the emotions his repressed nature had never been able to articulate or canalize.

At Oxford this concealed emotional sensitivity was still further complicated when he formed what can only be described as a half-romantic attachment for a fellow student, Moses Jackson, who had all the qualities making up the Greek ideal of perfect manhood. He was not only handsome, charming and athletic; he was also a brilliant scholar and of sterling moral character. Housman was dazzled by him, and although on the face of it they might seem to have had few tastes in common (Jackson was a scientist and Housman hopelessly unathletic) they became close friends. Whatever emotional undertones there may have been in the friendship on Housman's part, he might well have hidden it from the scrupulous Jackson who may nevertheless have had some inkling of the depth of Housman's regard for him if we can judge from the lines,

> Because I liked you better
> Than suits a man to say,

> It irked you, and I promised
> To throw the thought away.

Housman obtained a First in Moderations and then later came the inexplicable catastrophe of his life, his failure in Greats and the ruin of his academic career. How such an outstanding classical scholar could have ended his university life so ignominiously remains a mystery. One suggestion is that his previous academic successes had been obtained so easily that this had engendered a fatal over-confidence; another explanation is that he was seriously disturbed in his work by worries over the financial crisis then facing his family at home which his father was quite incapable of resolving. Only one certain fact is known about his last year at Oxford which may throw some light on the problem: during this time he shared rooms with Jackson, and so there existed between them a proximity and intimacy which could have distracted Housman and affected his capacity and will to work with the necessary dedication. Whatever the explanation of the *débâcle*, it embittered the rest of his life and gradually transformed him into a frustrated secretive recluse who rebuffed any attempt to penetrate his reserve.

He returned to Oxford for one term to qualify for a pass degree and then after a short spell of teaching he entered the Civil Service to become a Clerk in the Patent Office where Jackson was already employed. Moses Jackson shared bachelor lodgings with his young brother Adelbert, a lively young student who combined his elder brother's personal charm with literary tastes. Housman joined the *ménage* and remained with them for four years before moving into lodgings on his own. For some time he had been making a name for himself in the field of classical scholarship with a succession of articles in various learned journals on abstruse minutiae of textual problems, and he had already gained a reputation for the depth of his knowledge and for his merciless exposure of editorial inaccuracies. He still maintained his close friendship with the two Jacksons, but his ties with the elder were loosened when Moses Jackson married a young widow.

With Adelbert he continued to be on the same intimate terms until the young man's sudden death from typhoid, a tragedy which caused Housman much personal grief, and inspired the verses *A.J.J.*, one of the most intense expressions of his usually restrained emotion, and containing lines of bleak despair.

> Strange, strange to think his blood is cold
> And mine flows easy on,
> And that straight look, that heart of gold,
> That grace, that manhood gone.

After ten years at the Patent Office Housman applied for the vacant Chair of Latin at University College, London. It might have seemed an almost impudent presumption for a candidate with only a pass degree to apply for the appointment, but such was his reputation in his own narrowly specialized field, and so impressive were his testimonials that he was successful, and so began that association with academic life, first at London and then at Cambridge, which lasted until his death in 1936.

As a scholar Housman was respected and feared by both colleagues and students; his meticulous scholarship, his uncompromising devotion to accuracy, and his intolerance and merciless exposure of errors were allied to a caustic tongue and a forbidding manner of icy reserve. Whatever pent-up passions might lie behind that brusque exterior were kept well hidden until the slim volume of his verse, *A Shropshire Lad*, appeared in 1896. Here in forty-eight short poems written in a deceptively simple, artless lyrical style some of the repressed emotions found a circumscribed, guarded outlet. As Dr John Sparrow has remarked, we really cannot quite believe in the Shropshire lad's quarrels over Rose Harland, or the quaffing of Ludlow ale. The real theme of *A Shropshire Lad* is a romantic friendship between two young men; its consequent longing, regret and self-pity; and the two paradoxically opposed bitter complaints – that life is lovely but piteously brief, and that existence is an affliction from which death is a welcome deliverance –

Be still, be still, my soul; it is but for a season:
Let us endure an hour and see injustice done.

Some of the inspiration for Housman's poetry is factual. For example, in his own copy of the poems he kept a newspaper cutting about a young Woolwich cadet whose last letter before his suicide addressed to the coroner tells the tragedy of his own ruined life, and of his determination to choose this death rather than cause the moral ruin of another. In the same way the lad who 'sleeps in Shrewsbury jail' (No. IX); and the punishment of 'that young sinner' for something Housman felt could be blamed no more justifiably than 'the colour of his hair' (*Additional Poems* No. XVIII), suggest a foundation in fact. Many of the other poems, such as Nos XIV, XVIII, and XXIII of *A Shropshire Lad* bear the imprint of a more personal inspiration.

Originally the poems were to have been entitled *Poems by Terence Hearsay* which is the explanation of the otherwise meaningless appearance of the name 'Terence' in poems VIII and LXII. It was A. W. Pollard who made the inspired suggestion to Housman that *A Shropshire Lad* would make a much better title. In later years Housman explained that from his early childhood the Shropshire hills on the western border of his own county had always been a romantic horizon for him, but he admitted that apart from Ludlow and Wenlock he did not in fact know this countryside very well, and that in some of his poems some of the topographical details, for example those of Hughley and Abdon-under-Clee, were imaginary or inaccurate. Shortly after *A Shropshire Lad* was published, Housman's brother Laurence was staying at Buildwas and walked over to Hughley to look at the 'far-known' sign on Hughley steeple which his brother had written about. As we have already seen the 'steeple' is merely a small bell-turret, and there was yet another disillusionment for Laurence Housman: the graves of the 'slayers of themselves' on the north side of the churchyard were found in fact to be those of irreproachable churchwardens, and the respectable wives of former vicars.

But, after all, to romanticize a locality is only what Trollope did for Barsetshire and Thomas Hardy for Wessex, and this treatment of his setting in no way detracts from Housman's special appeal to those who know Shropshire.

Certain literary influences are easily traced in Housman's poetry; most especially there are reminiscences of the Border Ballads and Shakespeare's songs; and of Heine, Matthew Arnold and Stevenson; but there is nothing directly imitative about his style which is highly individual and immediately recognizable. For this reason the lyrics of *A Shropshire Lad*, like the novels of Mary Webb, have attracted a number of parodies. Among the best of them, as Housman himself admitted in a rare mood of laughing at himself, are Hugh Kingsmill's lines beginning,

> What, still alive at twenty-two,
> A clean, upstanding chap like you?
> Sure if your throat is hard to slit,
> Slit your girl's and swing for it

which neatly hit off both rhythm and style.

A Shropshire Lad was first printed and published at Housman's own expense, and it took two whole years to sell five hundred copies even at the low price of half a crown. Then during the 1914 war there was something of a boom in its sales, and the general popularity of Housman's poetry with the more discerning may be gauged by the number of composers who asked for permission to set verses of his to music. Ironically enough this was nearly always freely granted – ironically because Housman himself had no interest whatsoever in music, and was in fact tone-deaf. *Everyman's Dictionary of Music* lists settings of Housman's verses by no less than thirty-one composers, but perhaps the best-known are the song cycles of Vaughan Williams and of George Butterworth who also wrote an orchestral rhapsody called *A Shropshire Lad*. An amusing story is told that on one occasion someone wished to pay Housman a compliment by playing to him a recording of Gervase Elwes singing Vaughan Williams's song cycle of his poems. The result was as disastrous as it was un-expected; with an expression of mingled horror and anger Hous-man clapped his hands over his ears, and the record was hastily stopped.

In an essay on A. E. Housman written many years ago, but still valuable as an illuminating study of the writer, J. B. Priestley stressed that in Housman's poetry there is

something distinct, individual, personal. It is easy to write verse that is highly novel but not worth reading, as many people do; it is not very difficult to write verse that is quite readable but not original, as many others do; but to create lyrics that have certain rare literary qualities and, further, have their creator's personality clearly stamped on them, is to have some kinship with the great masters. A line from A. E. Housman is as unmistakable as a line from Milton, Shelley, or Wordsworth, and bears the same impress of the poet's individuality; and to me the difference between the modern poet and these three Titans, on this count of original force, is one of degree alone, for I hold him to be one of the same imperishable kind.

Some have argued that this unmistakable personal note of Housman's *A Shropshire Lad* might have been related equally effectively to any other locality, but for most of us there could have been only one region for his beacon on the 'high-reared' head of Clee; his Ludlow tower, chimes, market and fair; the mist from Teme; the gleaming vanes of Shrewsbury; the troubled wood on Wenlock Edge; and the heaving 'forest fleece' of the Wrekin – and they are now an integral part of the verses, and an indispens-able background to the poignant intensity of feeling which he expresses with such consummate artistic beauty, reticence and economy of words.

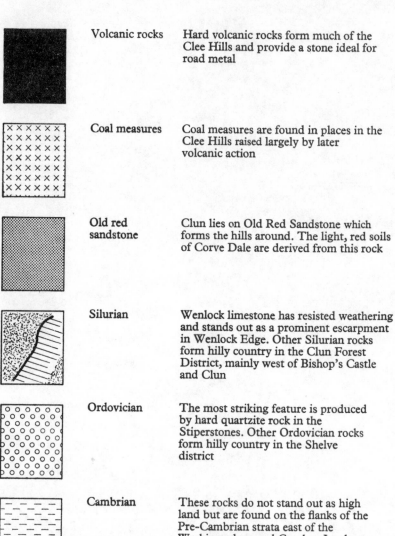

Volcanic rocks	Hard volcanic rocks form much of the Clee Hills and provide a stone ideal for road metal
Coal measures	Coal measures are found in places in the Clee Hills raised largely by later volcanic action
Old red sandstone	Clun lies on Old Red Sandstone which forms the hills around. The light, red soils of Corve Dale are derived from this rock
Silurian	Wenlock limestone has resisted weathering and stands out as a prominent escarpment in Wenlock Edge. Other Silurian rocks form hilly country in the Clun Forest District, mainly west of Bishop's Castle and Clun
Ordovician	The most striking feature is produced by hard quartzite rock in the Stiperstones. Other Ordovician rocks form hilly country in the Shelve district
Cambrian	These rocks do not stand out as high land but are found on the flanks of the Pre-Cambrian strata east of the Wrekin and around Comley. In places they contain Britain's earliest known fossils
Pre-Cambrian	These rocks form the Long Mynd, Ragleth Hill, Caer Caradoc, the Lawley and the Wrekin, but they extend over a much greater area between the Long Mynd and the Stiperstones

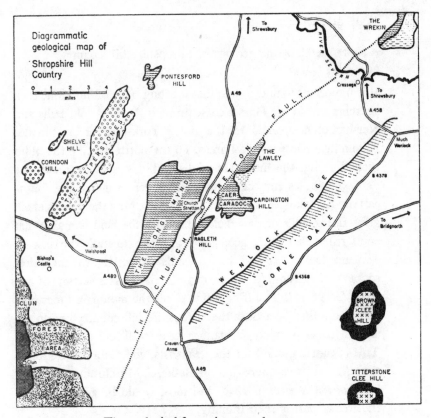

The geological formations are shown on
the diagrammatic map *only where they
give rise to an elevated tract of country*.

Appendix

A short sketch of the geology of Shropshire hill country
by A. W. Coysh

It is important to understand that the long ridge of limestone rock stretching from the Dorset coast through the Cotswold Hills and Northampton uplands to the north Yorkshire moors divides Britain into two geological areas. To the north-west lie the older rocks forming the mountains, hills and moors of Scotland, the Pennines, Wales and the south-western peninsula; to the south-east are the younger and softer rocks where only the porous chalk gives rise to hills or downland; otherwise the land is mainly flat and fertile. Therefore a geologist who wishes to study the rocks in sequence looks west – to the highlands of Scotland for the oldest rocks, to the Pennines or perhaps to the classic section of the Avon Gorge at Bristol if he wants to see the mountain limestone, and so on. But if he visits the Shropshire hill country he can see ancient rocks of many formations in a small and compact area. This is classic ground for the geologists, and Church Stretton is their Mecca. It was here that Sir Roderick Murchison established his *Silurian System* in 1839, and most would-be geologists visit the area as part of their training.

A sketch map is essential for an understanding of the rock sequence here, for there has been much folding and faulting, and centuries of weathering and erosion have produced the landscape outlines we know today. To the left of the map is a summary of the rock sequence which should be read upwards, starting with the oldest rocks and so working up through the rocks which overlie them. The first point to note is that a great crack in the earth's crust – a 'fault' – runs from just west of Craven Arms to Cressage on the Severn and beyond, passing a little to the east of Church Stretton on the way. It runs from south-south-west to north-north-east, and this is the general trend of most of the hill ridges. It is perhaps also useful to note that the main hill features have determined the routes taken by the main roads from the point where the A49 from the south reaches Craven Arms. Here the road to Much Wenlock and Bridgnorth branches to the north-east through Corve Dale, running parallel to the long limestone ridge of Wenlock Edge. A little farther to the north the road to Welshpool sweeps away to the north-west and is forced to curve round the southern spurs of the huge moorland plateau of the Long Mynd and the hard gritty ridge of the Stiperstones. The main road to Shrewsbury and the north passes east of the Long Mynd through Church Stretton, in the narrow valley between its eastern slopes and the broken ridge formed by Ragleth Hill and Caer Caradoc.

The oldest rocks of the Shropshire hill country are as old as any in Britain and belong to the Pre-Cambrian period. They are of two types. One type comprises rocks of volcanic origin (lava and ash) which give rise to a line of hills along the eastern side of the Church Stretton fault – Ragleth, Helmeth, Caer Caradoc and the Lawley – and which are continued north of the Severn in the Wrekin. There are also similar outcrops west of the fault, but Pontesford Hill is the only significant height. The other type is found in the Long Mynd, an extensive moorland area crossed by many small streams most of which flow eastwards in the steep-sided valleys known as 'batches'. This type consists of a massive thickness of sedimentary rocks, mainly shales, flagstones and conglomerates which were laid down under water and have since been tilted by earth movements so that the strata in many places are almost vertical.

The Cambrian rocks which follow in sequence are of very special interest since they contain the first recognizable evidence of life in the form of fossils. Some life may have existed before Cambrian times but there are no known remains. These rocks do not form high land but rest against the Pre-Cambrian on the flanks of Ragleth Hill, Caer Caradoc, the Lawley and the Wrekin. We owe much of our knowledge about them to a local geologist,

Dr E. S. Cobbold, who carried out detailed and scholarly research in the area between 1906 and 1936. He made a particular study of the fauna revealed by the fossils in the green sandstone at Comley, a small hamlet in the gap between Caer Caradoc and the Lawley. I well remember him from my student days when he conducted a party of geology students over the hills around Church Stretton, showing us the rock exposures he had found, and looking for fossils. Although he was then an old man he showed a vigour and enthusiasm which put us young students to shame. If we made an interesting find he would explain its significance in great detail; if he thought it might yield the smallest scrap of new material for his own researches he would ask to be allowed to take it home to his study for microscopic examination.

The Ordovician rocks, named after a Celtic tribe, follow the Cambrian and are best seen west of the Long Mynd. Among them is a hard quartzite rock which gives rise to the ridge of the Stiperstones. Farther west there are more ridges of hard rock in the Stiperstones area. Shales occur in the Ordovician sequence, and they often contain the fossilized remains of now extinct creatures trilobites and graptolites. There has also been volcanic action at some period which has thrust basaltic rocks through the strata with the mineral veins so often accompanying such activity. Lead was worked in the Stiperstones area by the Romans, and barytes and fluorspar are often found in the rocks.

The most striking feature of the next series, which Murchison named the Silurian after another Celtic tribe, is the limestone escarpment of Wenlock Edge running roughly from Craven Arms to Much Wenlock. It is full of fossil remains, notably of corals which are sometimes found in reef-like formation suggesting that the rocks were formed in much the same conditions as exist today along the Great Barrier Reef of Australia. The Edge has been extensively worked for lime from time to time and it is pitted with quarries. Silurian rocks also form hilly country in the south-west of Shropshire beyond Bishop's Castle and Clun to the River Teme which separates the area from the Welsh mountains. Much of this area is known as Clun Forest and it also contains the succeeding strata of the Old Red Sandstone period which are very different in character.

The period of open clear sea in which the coral limestones of Wenlock Edge were laid down was followed by earth movements which raised an east to west ridge across the South Wales area. This cut off an arm of the Silurian sea to form a huge lake covering much of Wales and its border country to the east, including the Shropshire area. At first the sandy and muddy deposits of this lake contained marine creatures with calcareous shells, and although the rocks formed were sandstone they contain some lime. That is why the rocks in the Clun Forest area break down in the valleys and flatter parts to form a soil which makes good farming land. Very soon, however, geologically speaking, conditions became entirely freshwater. In the relatively shallow lake, succeeding strata were formed which first produced red sandy rocks of the Silurian period, well seen at Ludlow, and then the true Old Red Sandstone on which the town of Clun is built. The Old Red Sandstone is also seen in Corve Dale east of Wenlock Edge.

The Coal Measures do not in themselves form hilly tracts of country, but the Clee Hills in places are capped by coal-bearing rocks raised to their present position by volcanic activity. Brown Clee and Titterstone Clee, in the south-east of the hill country, consist mainly of a dark basaltic lava, a very hard rock known commercially as 'dhu stone'. Vast quarries have eaten into the hills, and there are few roads in the Midlands which have not been metalled with this stone. Although, in a geological sense, these rocks are the youngest so far described, they were certainly formed long before the Ice Age when glaciers covered most of the Shropshire hill country. It was only when the ice retreated that man could move north and there are no signs of any prehistoric human settlements here before the Early Iron Age.

Index

Abdon Burf, 26, 40
Abdon-under-Clee, 144
Acton, Lord, 84
——, Sir John, 84
Acton Burnell, 8, 77
—— Scott 84
Afforestation, 110–12
All Stretton, 71–3, 88
Allcroft family, the, 58
Angel Bank, 38
Anger of the North, 130
Anglo-Saxon Chronicle, 102
Ape Dale, 52, 56–7
Armada, Spanish, 9–13
Armour Wherein He Trusted, 139
Arnold, Matthew, 145
Arthur, Prince, 9, 21, 36
Asterton, 97
Aston Munslow, 59
Auden, Thomas, 15
Avon Gorge, Bristol, 150

Badger Moor, 121
Bailey, E. H., 34
Baldwin, Joyce, 60

Baldwin, Stanley, 59, 139–40
——, Thomas, 58
Banwell, Somerset, 76
Bardsey Island, 45
Bath and Wells, Bishop of, 8, 76
Battlefield Church, 8
Beambridge, 61
Beeching, Lord, 69
Belême, Robert de, 6–7
Berkeley Castle, 34
Betrothed, The, 115–16
Bettws-y-Crwyn, 110, 121–2
Bishop's Castle, 98, 112, 114, 119, 124, 132, 152
—— Moat, 113
Bitterley, 38
Black Country, 27
Bladder Stone, the, 12–13
Blakeway Farm, Wenlock Edge, 52
'Bloody Mary', 9, 20–1
Bodbury Hill, 100
Boiling Well, 99
Botfield, Thomas, 33–4
Bouldon, 40
Brecon Beacons, 27

Breidden Hills, 3, 27
Bridges, 92, 100, 105
Bridgewater, Earl of, 21
Bridgnorth, 34, 151
Bristol, 150
—— Cathedral, 25, 76
Bromsgrove School, 140-1
Brook House, 121
—— Row, 32
Brookes, Dr William Penny, 48
Brown Clee, 26, 29, 41, 55, 100,
    153
Brown, William, 36
Bruere, Marion de la, 19, 21
Bryant, Arthur, 35
Bryn Mawr, 110
Buchan, John, 132
Bucknell, 3
Buildwas, 144
Builth, 8
Burne, Charlotte, 13, 91
Burne-Jones, Sir Edward, 30
Burnell, Sir Nicholas, 77
——, Robert, 76-7
Butterworth, George, 145
Byron, Lord, 83

Cader Idris, 27, 99
Caer Caradoc, 3, 71, 100, 151
Caesar, Julius, 2
Callow Hill, 57
Callowgate, 27
Cambridge, 75-6, 143
Canterville Ghost, The, 82
Cantlin, William, 121
Cantlin Cross and Stone, 121
Caractacus, 2-3
Caradoc (Caractacus), 2
Caradoc hills, see Stretton hills

Cardingmill Valley, 86-7, 90, 100
Cardington, 79-81, 83-4
—— Hill, 66
Carr, the Rev. Edmund Donald,
    88-92
Cartimandua, Queen, 3
Caynham, 30
Celtic Borderland, The, 47
Charles I, 44, 60, 78, 123-4
Charles II, Restoration of, 14, 117
Chaucer, Geoffrey, 107
Chester, 134
Chesterton, G. K., 127
Church Missionary Society, 75
Church Preen, 81
—— Stoke, 119
—— Stretton, 3, 55, 62, 70, 72, 84,
    87-8, 90, 97, 100, 111, 132,
    150-2
Churchman, William, 59
Churchtown, 108, 119
Civil War, the, 13-14, 30, 52,
    57-8, 117, 123-6
Clarendon, Earl of, 60
Claudius, Emperor, 3
Clayton, J., 130
Clee Burf, 26
—— Hills, the, 1, 18, 26, 28-33,
    37, 111, 139, 153
—— hill forts, 28
—— St Margaret, 41
Cleestanton, 27, 39
Clent Hills, 27
Cleobury Mortimer, 34-8
—— North, 39-40
Clive, Robert, 93-4
Clun, 112-19
—— Bridge, 115
—— Castle, 115-17

Clun Forest, 1, 98, 109, 119, 123, 153
—— —— Enclosure Act, 121
Cobbold, Dr E. S., 152
Coke, Edward, 118
Cold Comfort Farm, 135
Colebatch, 119
Coleridge, Samuel Taylor, 120
Colesty, 117
Colwall, parish of, 35
Comley, 152
Comus, 21
Cook, Ann, 65
Cookson, Judy, 49
Corbett family, the, 73
Corbett, Sir Richard, 74
Corely, 32–3
Corfil, Wm., 53
Corndon Hill, 99
Corve Dale, 27, 151, 153
——, River, 18, 45
Corvehill, William, 51
Cotswold Hills, 27, 150
Coubertin, Baron Pierre de, 48
Council of the Marches, 9, 14, 81
Court Lee, the, 59
Cove, R. N., xvii
Cow Hall, 122
Coxall Knoll, 3
Coysh, A. W., xvii, 2, 150
Craig Hill, 119
Cranberry Rock, 106
Craven Arms, 52, 56–7, 111, 150–2
Craven, Lord, 57
Creighton, Mandell, 15
Cressage, 150
Cromwell, Oliver, 79
Crookback, Richard, 9
Crossways, 121

Crown Inn, Munslow, 59, 119
Crowsnest, 107
Cwm Collo, 122
—— Ffrydd, 110, 120

Davies, the Rev. R. B., xvii
Dee, River, 4
Denbighshire Berwyns, 27
Devil's Causeway, the, 80–1
—— Chair, 28, 98, 101–2, 105, 132
—— Mouth, 100
Dew in April, 130
Dhu stone, 153
Dickens, Charles, 122
Diddlebury (Delbury), 58
Dilke, Charles, 118
Dinan, Joce de, 19
Domesday Book, 41, 54
Dorrington, 69
Drayton, Michael, 26

Earl's Hill, 102
Easthope, 54–5
Eaton (Eaton-under-Heywood), 56
Edenhope Hill, 120
Edric Sylvaticus (Wild Edric), 5–6
Edward I, 8, 76–7
Edward II, 34
Edward IV, 9, 20, 44
Edward V, 20
Elan valley lakes, 33
Elizabeth I, 58, 81, 110
Elwes, Gervase, 145
Ercall, the, 12–13
Ethelbert, King, 112

Falkner, Thomas, 95
Flounders, Benjamin, 57
Flounder's Folly, 57

Fockburg, 140
Forrest, H. E., 50
Foxe's *Book of Martyrs*, 80
Frog's Well, 81
Fuller, Thomas, 46
Funeral garlands, 107–8

Gaskell, Lady, 29, 97
Gaveston, Piers, 34
Geology of Shropshire hill country, 150–3
Giant's Chair, 28
Gibbons, Stella, 135
'Gliding Field', 97
Godiva, Lady, 45
Gold of Toulouse, 130
Golden Arrow, 102–3
Golden Arrow, The, 105, 127, 131–2
Gone to Earth, 132–4
Goodall, Frederick, 114
Grace Before Meat, 114
Graham, Stephen, 136
Griffiths, H., xvii
Grit Mine, 106
Groome, F. H., 29

Habberley, 103–4
Hadrian, Emperor, 3
Hall of the Forest, 122
Hampden, John, 60
Harcourt Manor, 128
Hardwick, Charles Espin, 98–9
Hardy, Thomas, 120, 136, 145
Haughmond Forest, 111
Hawkins, Canon D. F. C., xvii
Hayes, J. R., xvii
Hayward Forest, 21
Hazler Hill, 70–1

Heath Chapel, 40–1, 80
Heaven's Gate, 13
Heine, Heinrich, 145
Hell Gate, 13
—— Gutter, 101
Helmeth Hill, 70–1, 87, 151
Henry I, 6–7, 44
Henry III, 7, 44
Henry IV, 8
Henry V, 38
Henry VI, 24
Henry VII, 9, 20
Henry VIII, 9, 20, 46–7, 64, 107, 109
Hereford, Bishop of, 112–13
—— Cathedral, 112
Holloway Rocks, 123
Hope Bagot, 31–2
—— Dale, 57
——, manor of, 31
Hopesay Hill, 98
Hopton Castle, 123–6
—— Court, 33–4
—— Wafers, 33–4
Horne, Dom Ethelbert, 31
Hospital of the Holy and Undivided Trinity, 118
Hotspur, Harry, 8
House in Dormer Forest, The, 134–5
Housman, A. E., xvii, 25–7, 53, 127, 140–6
——, Laurence, 144
Howard, Henry (Earl of Northampton), 118
——, Sir Robert, 118
Hugh Gibbins Memorial Hostel, 92
Hughley, 53–4, 144
Hurricane Stone, 93

Ippikin's Rock, 54
Isabella, Queen, 34

Jackson, Adelbert, 142–3
——, Moses, 141–2
James I, 44, 78
James II, 71–3
James, Henry, 47, 52
Jessica's First Prayer, 65
John Inglesant, 96

Katherine of Aragon, 9, 20
Kenwealh, King of Wessex, 102
Kerry Forest, 111
Kingsmill, Hugh, 145
Kynaston, Wild Humphrey, 91

Lacy, Roger de, 6
——, Walter de, 19
Lacy family, the, 19
Langland, William, 34–5
Langley Chapel, 79–80
—— Hall, 79
Lawes, Henry, 21
Lawley, the, 71, 100, 151
Lawrence Hill, 12
Lea Castle, 113
Lead mining, 106–7
Lee, Sir Humphrey, 78
——, Richard, 74, 78
——, Samuel, 74–6
Leebotwood, 73
Leighton, 127–8
Leighton, Lord, 65
——, Sir William, 81, 83
Leofric, Earl of Mercia, 45
Leyland, John, 17, 28, 64, 110
Light Spout Waterfall, 86, 90
Linley Hall, 110

Linley Hill, 98
Lisle, Arnold de, 19, 21
Little Malvern Court, 96
—— Stretton, 62, 71
Littleton, Edward, 60–1
Llanfair Waterdine, 122–3
Long Forest, 111
Long Mountain, the, 99
Long Mynd, the, 1–2, 27, 52, 62,
        66, 70, 86–8, 91–3, 97–100,
        102, 132, 151–2
Longland, 35
Longmore, John, 32
Longnor, 74, 76
—— Hall, 74
Lower Dinchope, 57
Lucy, Sir Thomas, 38
——, Timothy, 38
Ludford Bridge, 17–18
Ludlow, 14, 17–27, 41, 153
—— Castle, 7, 9, 14, 18, 20, 30, 36
Ludlow Sketches, 86
Lydbury Castle, 112
—— North, 96–7
Lyth Hill, 134, 136

Macaulay, Lord, 9, 79, 83
Maesbrook, Meole Brace, 128
Mainstone, 109, 118–20
Major's Leap, 52, 54–5
Malmesbury, William of, 45–6
Malvern, 35
Malverns, the, 86
Manchester Grammar School, 95
Many Mansions, 43
Marcher Lords, the, 6–9, 34
Marchland, the, 109
Mare, Walter de la, 131, 136
Mary, Bloody, 9, 20–1

Mary, Queen of Scots, 58
Mary Webb, Her Life and Work,
127
Memoirs of the Life of John Mytton,
103
Memorials of Westminster, 22
Meole Brace, 128–9, 134
Meredith, George Edward, 127,
134
——, Gladys, 127–8, 134
Merry Wives of Windsor, the, 38
Midland Gliding Club, 98–9
Milburga, St, 41–2, 45–6
Milton, John, 21
Minshall, John, xvii
Minsterley, 107–8
Montfort, Simon de, 77
Montgomery, Roger de, 5–6, 45
Moor Hall, 122
Moore, Air Commodore L. P.,
xvii, 98
More, Colonel Samuel, 124–6
Mortimer Forest, 111
Mortimer, Hugh de, 19
——, Roger de, 34
Mortimer's Cross, battle of, 9
Mortimers of Ludlow, the, 9
Moult, Thomas, 127–8
Mount Pleasant, 122
Much Wenlock, 5, 41, 43–52, 58,
61, 128, 150, 152
Munsloe, Richardus Baldwin de, 59
Munslow, 59–60
Murchison, Sir Roderick, 101, 150,
152
Myndtown, 93, 97
Mytton, John, 103–4
——, William, 103
Mytton's Beach, 107

National Trust, 55
Needle's Eye, 12–13
Nelson, Lord, 34
New House Farm, 71
Newcastle, village of, 119
Night in the Snow, A, 89, 91
Nills, the, 132, 134
Nipstone Rock, 106
Nordy Bank, 26, 41
Norman Conquest, 4
Norris, Thomas, 83
Northumberland, Duke of, 70
Nottingham, 123
Nubian Slave, The, 114

Offa, King, 4, 112
Offa's Dyke, 99, 109, 119, 120, 122
——, Path, 4
Olympic Games (1896), 48
Onny, River, 57, 93
Orewyn Bridge, 8
Overdale, 71
Oxford, 140, 142

Paganel, Gervase, 7
Penda, King (of Mercia), 42, 102
Pendower Tower, 19
Pengwern, 4
Pennerley, 107
Pennines, the, 150
Percys, the, 8
Perkin's Beach, 107
Petition of Right, 60
Pevsner, Professor Nikolaus, 18,
47, 81–2, 123
Phillips, Major, 124–6
Phiz, 122
Piers Plowman, 34–5
Plaish Hall, 81–2

Plautius, Aulus, 2
Plowden, 93, 97, 99
—— Chapel, 96
—— Hall, 94–6
—— Woods, 93
Plowden, Edmund, 94–5
——, Roger, 96
Plynlimon, 99
Pollard, 144
Pontesbury, 102, 130
Pontesford, 103
—— Hill, 102, 130, 151
Portraits of Places, 47
Portway, the, 86, 99
Posentesbyrig, 102
Potter's Pit, 106
Pound Inn, the, 73
Powis family, the, 110
Precious Bane, 137–8
Priestley, J. B., xvii, 146
Princes in the Tower, 20–1
Priory School, Shrewsbury, the,
    134
Prolley Moor, 97

Quantock Hills, 86

Radnor Forest, 27
Ragleth Hill, 70–1, 151
—— Inn, the, 62–4
Raising the Maypole, 114
Ratlinghope, 88, 92, 100, 132
Raven's Bowl, the, 12–13
Rea Brook, valley of the, 102
Restoration, the, 14, 117
Rice, Griffin Ap, 37
Richard II, 44
Richard III, 9
Rivers, Lord, 20

Robin Hood's Butts, 91
Rokayle, Eustace de, 34–5
Romans in Shropshire, 2–3
Rose Cottage, Pontesbury, 130, 132
Roses, Wars of the, 9
Roseville, Pontesbury, 130
Rowse, A. L., 51–2
Ruckley, 80
Rupert, Prince, 125
Rushbury, 56, 61

St Leonards-on-Sea, 139
St Milburga, 41–2
St Milburga's Abbey, 45–6
St Owen, 44
St Owen's Well, 44, 50
Sandford Avenue, 71
Say, Robert de, 6
Scapula, Ostorius, 2
Scattered Rock, 105
Scott, Sir Walter, 115–17
Seven for a Secret, 136–7
Severn, River, xv, 1, 12–13, 76,
    150–1
Shadwell Hall, 119
Shakespeare, William, 38, 63, 145
Sharpstones, 66
Sheila-na-gig, 64
Ship Money dispute, 60
Shipton Hall, 61
Shorthouse, J. H., 96
Shrewsbury, 4–8, 12–13, 71–2,
    102–4, 130, 134, 140, 146,
    151
——, Benedictine Abbey of, 5
—— Castle, 7, 14
—— and Hereford railway, 68–70
Shropshire Archaeological Society,
    59

Shropshire Folklore, 13, 91
Shropshire Lad, A, xvi, 53, 127,
   140–1, 143–6
Shropshire Light Infantry, 15
Siefton Batch, 56
Silurian System, 150
Skyrrid Fawr, 27
Small Batch, 62
Smallman family, the, 55
Smallman, Thomas, 52
Smith, Sarah, 64
Snail Beach, 106
Snell, F. J., 47, 116
Snowdonia, 99
Sparrow, Dr John, 143
Spring Cottage, 134, 136
Spring in a Shropshire Abbey, 97
Spring of Joy, the, 128–9
Springhill, 122
Stanley, Dean, 22
Stanton-on-Hine Heath, 128
Stapeley Hill, 99
Stephen, King, 19
Stevenson, R. L., 85, 145
Stiperstones, the, 1–5, 28, 52, 97,
   99, 101–2, 105–6, 132,
   151–2
—— Forest, 111
Stoke St Milborough, 41, 45
Stokesay Castle, 57–8
Stone, Nicholas, 78
Stoneacton, 84
Stoney Pound, 122
Stow, 123
Stretton, Hesba, 64–5
Stretton hills, 1, 3, 27, 40, 52, 62,
   70–1, 100
—— private asylum, 67
Sutton, Major, 125

Sylvaticus, Edric, 5
Symons, Robert E., xvii
*Synoptic History of the Midland
   Gliding Club, A*, 98

Tacitus, 2–3
Talbot, C. R., xvii
Teme, River, 18, 123, 146, 152–3
Thomas, A. L., xvii
Three Gates, 119
Thynne, Sir John, 107
——, William, 107
Ticklerton, 84
Timperley, H. W., 12, 87
Tired Soldiers, the, 114
Titterstone Clee, 26–8, 153
Tower of London, 9, 58
Trevelyan, G. M., xv
Trollope, Anthony, 145

Under the Greenwood Tree, 120
Underhill, Evelyn, 136
Unk, River, 119
Upper Hill Farm, 54

Vassons, 106
Vaughan Williams, R., 145
Viroconium, 2–4, 76
Voysey, J. C., xvii

Waffre, Robert le, 33
Walcot, 93–4
—— Chapel, 97
—— Forest, 111
—— Hall, 110
Walcot, John, 38–9
Wall Bank, 84
Watling Street, 71
Webb, H. B. L., 129–30, 132, 134,
   136, 138

Webb, Mary, xvi, xvii, 43, 102, 105, 127–32, 134–40, 145
Wellington, Duke of, 70
Wells, 76–7
Welshpool, 151
Wenlock Edge, 1, 6, 18, 27, 40, 52–7, 66, 79, 100, 144, 146, 151–3
Wenlock, John, 44
Wenlock Olympian Society, 48
—— Priory, 46, 54–5
Wentnor, 92–3, 97
Westhope, 56–7
Weston, 109
Weston-super-Mare, 102, 129–30
Whinberries, 91–2
Whitcliffe, 17, 19
White, Walter, 39, 43, 65
Whitton, 30
Wild Edric, 5–6, 101
Wilde, Oscar, 82

Wilderhope Manor, 52, 55
William the Conqueror, 4–6, 46
William of Malmesbury, 45
William Rufus, 6
Willstone, 71
Windsor, George R., 67–8
Woodhouse, Sir Michael, 125
Woolstaston, 88, 91, 99
Worcester, 36, 72
—— Cathedral, 24
Wrekin, the, 1, 9–13, 27, 40, 55, 76, 100, 127, 146, 151
Wrenn, Dorothy P. H., 128
Wright, Thomas, 86
Wroxeter, 2
Wulfhere, 102
Wye, River, 4
Wyre Forest, 27

Youth Hostel Association, 55